Books by the same author:

Discovering How to Pray

Discovering the Joy of Obedience
Traditional Values For Today's New Woman

When Angels Appear

HOPE MACDONALD

Zondervan Publishing House
Grand Rapids, Michigan

WHEN ANGELS APPEAR
Copyright © 1982 by Hope MacDonald
Grand Rapids, Michigan

Requests for information should be addressed to:
Zondervan Publishing House
Grand Rapids, Michigan 49530

Library of Congress Cataloging in Publication Data
MacDonald, Hope.
    When angels appear.

    1. Angels.   I. Title.
BT966.2.M24   1982   235'.3   82-15908
ISBN 0-310-28531-3

Edited by Julie Ackerman Link
Designed by Louise Bauer

Printed in the United States of America

93   94   95 / CH / 18

To my grandchildren,
my earthly angels,

Breelyn Rose MacDonald
Scott Benjamin MacDonald Gronholz
Megan Cherie MacDonald
Shane Matthew MacDonald Gronholz
Jenny Kathleen MacDonald
Skye Marc MacDonald Gronholz

Acknowledgments

I want to thank my husband, Harry MacDonald, for his constant encouragement and faithful prayers during the time I wrote this book. I would also like to thank the praying family of the John Knox Presbyterian Church of Seattle for their prayers and loving support.

I would never attempt writing a book without a small group of committed, praying friends. These people prayed for me faithfully until the book was completed. The inspiration and help I received from them are much a part of this book.

Denise Adler	Pat Kelly
Mildred Burt	Helen Leonard
Barbara Diamond	Margaret Logan
Eva Engholm	Marilyn Mead
Jean Griffin	Beverly Miller
Madalene Harris	Jane Short

My special heartfelt thanks go to the hundreds of people who took time to freely share their angel stories with me. Without them, there would be no book called *When Angels Appear*.

Contents

Part 1

ABOUT ANGELS

About Angels

MY FIRST ENCOUNTER with an angel happened when I was four years old. My sister Marilyn was eight at the time and my parents had driven her to school that day. An hour later I watched as they carried her back into the house covered with blood and bruises. They laid her on the couch until the doctor arrived. In attempting to cross the street near school that morning, she had darted into the path of an oncoming car and had been thrown twenty feet into the air. When she hit the pavement, my parents watched helplessly as she rolled full speed toward a large, uncovered, open sewer. But instead of falling in, as everyone expected, she suddenly stopped, right at the edge of the sewer. Later my parents related this story to the doctor. They all shook their heads in amazement. How could she have stopped so suddenly, at the very edge of the sewer, when she had been rolling so fast? In a voice filled with surprise, my sister spoke up from the couch and said,

"But didn't you see that huge, beautiful angel standing in the sewer, holding up her hands to keep me from rolling in?"

I have never forgotten that incident from my childhood, even though it happened many years ago. Three years ago I decided I would do some research on the subject. I began to ask people every place I went if they had ever seen an angel.

My first story came not long after, when my husband and I were having dinner in Washington, D.C. I asked our friends at the table if anyone knew an angel story. All of them said no, but a very interesting conversation followed that question. (It always does!) By the time we were served dessert, Bob, who was sitting across the table from me said, "Yes, Hope, I have an angel story."

That was the beginning. These past three years, every place I go and each time I speak around the country, I always ask if anyone has an angel story. The surprising thing is that in every group, whether there are five people or one thousand people, there is usually someone who has a story to tell me. They often start out by saying, "Well, this may not be what you are looking for but. . . ." And then they proceed to tell their story. Most of them have three things in common: they had never shared their story with anyone before; they felt the experience had made a great difference in their lives; and they all thanked me for giving them the opportunity to share their angel story.

The stories in this book were chosen from hundreds I collected during these past three years from people in every walk of life. Some are from presidents of large firms, others are from dentists, pastors, missionaries, homemakers, students, and various other career people. They are all from intelligent, sophisticated people. I am convinced that these stories are real experiences from these people's lives. You will be strengthened and encouraged, as I was, as you read how God ministered to them by sending His angels.

Along with interviewing people, I knew it was imperative that I read all the books I could find about angels. Can you imagine my surprise when I walked into one of the finest bookstores in Chicago and discovered only two books on the subject? I found this to be true in every bookstore I visited. The most I could come up with in my entire search for books on angels was eight books.

Yet in this same search, I discovered hundreds of books about the devil, demons, witchcraft, and the occult. Entire sections of bookstores were devoted to them. I was surprised that so much had been written about the devil and his domain and so little had been written about God's angels.

I noticed this same phenomenon as I traveled around the world. While in Scotland last summer, my husband and I visited one of the larger bookstores. We discovered shelf after shelf of books about the devil and the occult, but not one book in the entire store about angels.

Our movies and television screens abound with stories of demon possession. Rock groups insidiously take up the same refrain. One of the top songs on all the charts not long ago was entitled "Sympathy for the Devil."

What has happened to produce such a morbid curiosity in the occult? It has been estimated that there are over two hundred fifty thousand witches in the United States alone. Some universities now offer classes in witchcraft. When I attended school, science was the golden calf. We were taught to believe only what we could see and dissect. Where has all this macabre interest in the occult come from?

I believe that the drug culture, which sprang up in our country in the 60s, prepared the way for the occult as we know it today. There is simply no way we could have gone from the happy-go-lucky days of the 50s into the senseless insanity of the occult in the 70s, without the way being paved by the satanic drug culture. And if, as many theologians believe, the return of Jesus Christ is at hand and the Antichrist is possibly alive today, this could be one reason why the power of evil is so strong.

As the popularity of the occult has increased, our eyes have been blinded to the great biblical truth of the reality of God's angels. Hardly anyone mentions them today. Rarely is a sermon preached on them or a book written about them. When they are mentioned, it is often with the skepticism of the Middle Ages, when scholars spent their time trying to figure out how many angels could dance on the head of a pin! Mohammed said that an angel accompanies every raindrop. Today angels are often thought of as fairies, elves, goblins or leprechauns. Or, they are pictured as some sort of medieval court jesters who play tricks on people from time to time.

We must get our eyes off the devil and turn them back to the great supernatural God of the Bible. God's ministering angels are at work in the world today. They are at work in our lives as believers. Billy Graham, in his book on angels, says, "Angels have a much more important place in the Bible than the devil and his demons."[1] The references in the Bible to angels far outnumber the references to the devil. Angels are mentioned over three hundred times. The Bible is full of dramatic angelic appearances and deliverances. It teaches that angels intervene on our behalf. God uses angels to change history, such as the time He sent the plagues in Egypt. In Genesis 19 we read how the cities of Sodom and Gomorrah were destroyed by angels sent from God. And many of our lives have been altered, usually without our knowing it, as an angel reached out and ministered to us in some special way for the glory of God.

ANGELS ARE BIBLICAL

We believe in angels today because the Bible explicitly teaches they exist. It lists story after story of extraordinary, supernatural events, simply presented in two or three phrases. Each word speaks for itself in life-changing sentences.

But what do the angels do? What do they look like? Recently, in talking about this to a friend with three teenage sons, she said with a chuckle, "A few years ago we thought we had given birth to three angels—now we know differently!" The Bible doesn't go into a detailed description of angels. It simply teaches that they exist. But we can't help wondering at times what they look like. As I sorted through the many angel stories I have collected, I discovered most of them did not describe what the angel they encountered looked like. Apparently that didn't seem important in relating their story. Then I remembered my husband, Harry, and I saw an angel many years ago and we too have never attempted to describe how it looked in physical terms.

This is how our angel story happened. We were engaged and planned to be married the following summer. Harry was attending seminary several hundred miles from my home. During spring break, I took a bus and went to visit him for a week. I stayed in the home of a lady he knew who was in full-time Christian work. She was a dynamic woman of God and greatly respected by all. Yet somehow, we didn't get along together too well. I was very shy and found it difficult to think of anything important to talk about with her. The day before I was to return home, she sat down with Harry and told him he ought to seriously reconsider his decision to marry me. She felt I was too quiet and immature and that I could possibly ruin his ministry. Coming from someone he respected so much, this greatly disturbed Harry.

That night Harry and I went out for dinner with Beverly, a school friend of mine I hadn't seen for several years. Beverly and I got very silly as we reminisced together about old friends and experiences. It seemed we laughed through the whole dinner. Later in the evening we went bowling. This turned into a real disaster because Harry is an excellent bowler, and Beverly and I seemed to throw more balls in the gutter than we did down the lane! Each gutter ball sent us howling with laughter. And there was Harry, looking at me in light of what he had been told that morning, and he didn't think anything about the entire evening was very funny.

I knew by the time we reached the house where I was staying that he was greatly troubled about something. He returned to his small attic room and spent a sleepless night in prayer. He knew God had called him into the ministry and it was important to have the right woman as his life partner. Was I really the one for him? Was I too shy? Was I too immature?

Our last day together we had a picnic in one of the lovely parks near his seminary. The air was filled with the sunshine of a summer morning, and the gardens were alive with a rainbow of flowers. But a dark shadow seemed to have fallen on our day. I knew something was wrong. After we finished our lunch, he began to share his troubled thoughts with me. We spent most of the afternoon walking through the park and talking about these new problems that had arisen in our relationship. In the end, I felt it only fair to return the engagement ring until he had more time to think it over. I never dreamed he would take the ring back, but he did. As he put it in his pocket, my heart grew cold and heavy. I knew that when I got on the bus and returned to my hometown, I would never see him again.

Somehow we got through the dinner his landlady prepared for us that night. Just before he was to drive me to the bus station, he said, "Let's pray about this once more." And we went upstairs into the cold attic room where he lived. He knelt down on one side of the bed and I knelt on the other. And with sad, troubled hearts, we began to pray. As we prayed, suddenly the room was filled with a majestic presence and a force of energy so strong we both felt it. Harry stopped right in the middle of his prayer and we both looked over toward the door. There we saw a gloriously shining figure standing by the open door. A sense of quietness, filled with worship and glory, fell upon us. The figure moved slowly across the room and stood at the foot of the bed with outstretched arms. We felt the gentle touch of God's blessing upon us like a breath of warm sunshine. A soft glow of loving light seemed to permeate the room, and a feeling of great tenderness flowed from the presence. We didn't hear any audible voice, but a strong sense of communication passed between us, assuring us that God wanted us together. No words were needed. We understood the message clearly. And then the figure was gone, and we were left with a warmth and peace so deep in our hearts that it has never left us, even though that happened thirty-four years ago.

What did the angel look like? I don't know. We were only aware of an eternal presence bathed in a pearly white glow of splendor. And although no voice was heard, the light communicated to our souls the message that God's hand of blessing was on our lives together. There has never been a doubt in either of our minds about what happened in that little attic room so long ago. We never questioned if we had seen an angel or if the presence was real. We knew in our hearts it was real. It had happened.

WHO ARE ANGELS?
WHAT ARE THEY LIKE?

Angels are created beings. They did not always exist (Col. 1:16). They are dignified, majestic, intelligent beings, and we must take them seriously. They are responsible only to God and are under His direct orders. They are spiritual beings who cannot normally be seen with the human eye. However, they can be both visible and invisible and often appear as exceedingly beautiful. Angels are personal beings

17

who represent God. But they cannot be everywhere at once. They are not omnipresent. Only God is.

In the story of Adam and Eve, God placed an angel at the entrance of the Garden of Eden to keep them from returning. Angels have always had an important place in God's universe and a significant task to do here on earth.

Revelation describes them as being clothed in white robes with golden sashes. Another is described as being "robed in a cloud with a rainbow over his head" (Rev. 10:1). Père Lamy (1853–1931), a simple French priest, describes angels like this:

> Their garments are white, but with an unearthly whiteness. I cannot describe it, because it cannot be compared to earthly whiteness; it is much softer to the eye. These bright angels are enveloped in a light so different from ours that by comparison everything else seems dark. When you see a band of fifty you are lost in amazement. They seem clothed with golden plates, constantly moving, like so many suns.[2]

Many times an angel takes on the physical form of a person and is sometimes mistaken for a human being. "Do not forget to entertain strangers, for by so doing some people have entertained angels without knowing it" (Heb. 13:2).

I have often wondered if the little beggar girl and her mother who came to my gate one hot summer day in Brazil were angels. It was such a strange experience. I remember sitting at our dining room table in São Paulo, writing a monthly article to send to all the people in America who supported our work. As I was deep in thought, I heard the loud clapping of hands at my front gate. Most houses in Brazil do not have door bells and this was the way people "knocked" at your door. With a very annoyed sigh I went out to the gate. Standing there was a little girl about twelve years old with her mother. They were very dirty and ragged and covered with many running sores. They asked for a drink of water. In all the years we served as missionaries in

18

Brazil, I never turned a beggar away from the gate. Yet I was impatient to get my article finished. Thinking that a neighbor would give them a drink, I sent them away. No sooner had I sat down at the table to continue my writing then an inner thought came to me loud and clear: "You have turned away two angels!" I sprang up from my chair, ran out the door to the gate, and called after them; but they were gone. I dashed into the dusty road and looked frantically up and down the street. It was empty. How could that be? They couldn't have walked even to the next house in those few seconds. Yet they were gone, and I was left with a dreadful feeling of deep loss. Were they angels in human form sent to teach me a lesson I would never forget? Was writing an article really more important than giving a cup of cold water in the name of Jesus?

WHAT ANGELS DO

In this book, our main interest is not what angels are or what they look like, but rather what they do. How did they act in biblical days and how do they minister to us today?

The word angel means messenger. As God's messengers, "They are cast as working behind the scenes in the drama of world events as agents of God to promote His program. They execute His judgements and convey His blessings."[3] Angels are never spoken of in the Bible in vague, mystical ways. They are real and they have an authentic job to do. "Praise the Lord, you his angels, you mighty ones who do his bidding, who obey his word" (Ps. 103:20). Their primary purpose is to serve God, to worship and to praise Him. "Praise him, all his angels, praise him, all his heavenly hosts." (Ps. 148:2). "Let all God's angels worship Him" (Heb. 1:6).

The angels protected Jesus when He was a baby. They strengthened Him at His hour of temptation. They ministered to Him in the garden, and thousands of them were available to rescue Jesus from those who took Him to the cross (Matt. 26:53). The angels rolled the stone away from the garden tomb and announced His resurrection. They sat in the empty tomb and asked a question that still rings down to us today. "Why do you seek the living among the dead? He is not here, He is risen" (Luke 24:5, 6). And all history from that moment on would never be the same.

The angels who announced His birth to the shepherds on that starry night in Bethlehem, also announced His second coming. They (the disciples) were looking intently up into the sky as He was going, when suddenly two men dressed in white stood beside them. "Men of Galilee," they said, "Why do you stand here looking into the sky? This same Jesus, who has been taken from you into heaven, will come back in the same way you have seen him go into heaven" (Acts 1:10, 11). The angels will come with Jesus when He comes back the second time in all His power and glory. "When the Son of Man comes in His glory, and all the angels with him, he will sit on his throne in heavenly glory" (Matt. 25:31). They will gather in God's children from all over the earth. "And he will send his angels with a loud trumpet call, and they will gather his elect from the four winds, from one end of the heavens to the other" (Matt. 24:31). And the great, mighty angelic host will encircle the throne and sing "Worthy is the Lamb who was slain, to receive power and wealth and wisdom and strength and honor and glory and praise!" (Rev. 5:12).

How many angels does the heavenly host have? We don't know for sure and it really isn't important. We do know that when Jesus was arrested He told Peter He could call twelve legions of angels to deliver Him (Matt. 26:53). A legion was six thousand soldiers in that day, which would equal seventy-two thousand angels. Daniel tells us there are ten thousand times ten thousand. And Revelation says that there are thousands upon thousands.

We know that angels are God's representatives. They

are messengers ordered by God to minister to us in countless ways. They protect us time after time in ways we are not even aware of. None of us has any idea how many times an angel has stepped in to protect us. I believe when we get to heaven and look back at our days here on earth, we are going to be surprised at how many times God sent His angels to protect and deliver us from harm and danger. And how often we were comforted, unknowingly, by their gentle ministry. Most of us will probably never see an angel here on earth, but we can recognize the results of their care and protection.

When our son-in-law, Marc Gronholz, was seventeen years old, he was struck by a speeding station wagon one day while riding his bicycle to work. As Marc fell, he rolled into the path of the back wheel of the car. The car drove over his back and continued down the street. Passersby stopped to help Marc and couldn't believe he was all right. After a brief visit at the hospital where x-rays revealed no broken bones, Marc continued on his way to work—with big black tire marks across the back of his shirt! Surely his guardian angel had protected him.

> For He will command His angels concerning you to guard you in all your ways; they will lift you up in their hands, so that you will not strike your foot against a stone (Ps. 91:11, 12).

When I was thirteen years old, I used to look forward with great anticipation to Saturday night. I would take my carefully guarded fifteen cents and buy a small bag of potato chips and a bottle of Pepsi. (Now you know how long ago that was!) Later in the evening, I would fill the bathtub to the very top with mountains of radiant bubbles. I would turn on my little radio to my favorite program, "The Hit Parade," and settle down in the tub with my goodies for a nice hour's soak. As I munched my potato chips one particular Saturday night, my favorite song came on. In order to hear it better, I reached over to the stool my radio was sitting on and touched the dial. Instantly the bathroom was filled with a sizzling cobalt blue light. Zigzags of lightning came from the radio and froze my hand to the dial. Somehow, amid the loud hissing sound of electricity passing through the air, I was able to pull my hand free. I was left shaking all over for quite a while and with a very sore arm for several weeks. Since that time I have occasionally read in the newspapers of people being killed in the bathtub by touching the dial of their radio. I didn't see any angel that night, yet I believe one reached out and rescued me from the electrical current.

God often provides us with unique protection through His angels. "My God sent his angel, and he shut the mouths of the lions. They have not hurt me" (Dan. 6:22). Angels protect and deliver God's people. They guard our bodies and direct us in the right path. They open our eyes to sudden danger and help us in our physical weakness. They encourage us and minister to us in times of distress and need. They opened prison doors for Peter, directed Phillip to a new ministry, and gave very specific directions to Cornelius (Acts 12:5–11; 8:26; 10:1–7).

When we choose to receive Jesus as Lord and Savior, we also receive the faithful protection and care of the angels. This could limit guardian angels to only the believers, rather than to every person on earth. "Are not all angels ministering spirits sent to serve those who will inherit salvation?" (Heb. 1:14). We don't know for sure but it is possible that as Christians, we are assigned a special angel to guard and protect us. Charles Wesley wrote:

> Angels, where'er we go,
> Attend our step whate'er betide.
> With watchful care their charge defend,
> And evil turn aside.

Even though God sends His angels to protect us in various ways, we must still be aware of the difference between the work of the angels in our lives and the ministry of the Holy Spirit. The Holy Spirit is the all-powerful, omnipresent, third person of the Trinity. He is the guardian of our souls and He ministers to us spiritually, while angels minister to us physically. The Holy Spirit dwells within us and seals us with His guarantee that we really do belong to the family of God (Eph. 1:13, 14). He intercedes on our behalf and convicts us of sin. He teaches us, guides us and comforts us. The Holy Spirit ministers *in* us and the angels minister *to* us. Above all else, the Holy Spirit points us always and continually to Jesus.

This is one thing the angels have in common with the Holy Spirit. Their purpose is to direct us to Jesus Christ and never to themselves. It is always God's message they convey to us. It is always His help and protection they bring.

TWO DANGERS TO AVOID

There are two areas of danger that we need to be aware of in our thinking about angels.

First, at no time should we ever worship them. The Bible warns us time after time not to worship any created being. God alone is worthy of our worship and adoration. We must never become angel-centered in our worship, only God-centered.

> I, John, am the one who heard and saw these things. And when I had heard and seen them, I fell down to worship at the feet of the angel who had been showing them to me. But he said to me, "Do not do it! I am a fellow servant with you and with your brothers the prophets and of all who keep the words of this book. Worship God! (Rev. 22:8, 9).

Entire cults have been founded on the worship of angels. The early church may have experienced this type of problem because Paul warned against the danger of angel worship. In 325 A.D., the council of Nicaea made belief in angels a part of the Christian dogma. This produced a whole new wave of angel worship. We need to be aware that this could happen in our lives even today. We must never put our faith in angels, but only in the great sovereign God of the Bible. Angels are simply a demonstration of God's great love and care for us. Their total devotion and obedience to God is an example to us. They always respond to God's commands out of complete love for Him.

Second, we do not pray to angels. We can ask God to send an angel to help or minister to someone, and this knowledge should give us great comfort and encouragement. But we do not pray to them. When our children are driving home from college on icy roads, it is reassuring to know we can ask the God of creation to send a guardian angel to keep them from harm or danger. We can ask God to send a ministering angel to stand at the bedside of a suffering loved one. This is all part of the awesome privilege we have as God's children. But we must never pray to angels themselves.

Let's ask God to give us a healthy balance in regard to His angels. It is necessary and important that we believe in angels because the Bible gives us abundant evidence, from the beginning to the end, that they exist. Jesus referred to them often in His earthly ministry. There isn't any room for disbelief. We cannot brush them off the pages of history or out of our everyday lives on the pretense of imagination or fantasy. Angels exist. They are real. They are sent by God to help us.

But Lord, Where Was My Angel?

As I SIT AT MY TYPEWRITER this morning, watching the warm sunshine play across the green leaves of our maple trees, I am thinking about all of you reading this book who did not have an angel to help you through a difficult experience. Maybe your child was killed in a fall or in an automobile accident and you are asking, "But Lord, where was my angel?"

I remember the story of Daniel in the lions' den. God miraculously sent an angel to shut the lions' mouths. Yet a few hundred years later, thousands of Christians were devoured by the hungry lions in the Roman Colosseum. Does this mean God loved Daniel more than those new faithful Christians?

What about Shadrach, Meshach, and Abednego when King Nebuchadnezzar had them thrown into the fiery furnace? (Dan. 3:19–30). The Bible tells us not one hair of their heads was even singed as an angel came and walked around in the fire with them, protecting them from the roaring flames. Still I remember when I was in eighth grade, my very best girlfriend, Joann Johnson, was burned to death in her home along with her two brothers. Where was the angel to protect them? Didn't God love Joann as much as He loved Shadrach, Meshach, and Abednego?

Or how about Elijah? He was out in the wilderness for days without any food to eat. He was weak from hunger and laid down to sleep (1 Kings 19:5–9). While he was sleeping, an angel came and baked him a cake and gave him enough food and water to last for forty days. But where was the angel, and where was the cake for the little starving boy I saw on television news last night?

Where was the angel when my friend's three teenage children were suddenly killed by a train at an unmarked railroad crossing?

No one has the answers to these questions. Most of the time there isn't any answer. We know that during the days when Jesus lived on earth, He didn't heal every blind, sick, and crippled person in the entire city of Jerusalem. He didn't stand at the entrance of each tomb and call every person back to life as He did Lazarus. When you read through your Bible, you find that God did intervene in certain circumstances; but those circumstances were the exception, not the rule. God does send some angels to rescue His people from time to time, but those instances are rare. We remember that only three of the twelve disciples saw the glowing garments of Jesus when He appeared with Moses and Elijah on the Mount of Transfiguration (Matt. 17:3). The other nine did not have that heavenly experience. Yet they continued to love and serve Him and even died for Him in the same way as the three disciples who had had that encounter.

We must remember God has hundreds of different ways to minister to us in our times of need. Sometimes it is through an angel, but most of the time it is through the quiet certainty within our hearts that He is with us. Perhaps during our journey here on earth, an angel will appear briefly; but it will happen quickly, like a flash of silver moonlight that is soon covered by a cloud on a summer night. And we must remember that those who experience this are no more blessed than others who face the same situation and receive no vision of glory.

When dealing with the question "Where was my angel?" we must remember that all creation is affected by the fall and that, as a result, we live in a sin-filled world. And we must recognize the truth that every person, at one time or another, will face sickness, heartache, suffering, and death. We remember that our faith and trust is not in a visible angel or in some miraculous deliverance, but in God alone. We rest in the knowledge that God may not always be understood, but He can *always* be trusted.

When we come up against the sudden loss of a loved one, the suffering of a prolonged, incurable disease, or a tragic accident, we are faced with the undeniable truth that Satan's power is still strong in our world.

Yet God can use these adversities in our lives to strengthen our faith and make us strong, mature believers. He can take the broken pieces of our sorrow and make something beautiful and meaningful. He often uses these tragic experiences to teach us to comfort others who must walk down the same trail we have walked. He can also use these experiences to turn us away from the road that leads to destruction and point us back to the pathway that leads to fellowship with Him. "For God sometimes uses sorrow in our lives to help us turn away from sin and seek eternal life" (2 Cor. 2:7–11 LB). God takes what Satan meant for harm and makes something good out of it.

> We can rejoice, too, when we run into problems and trials for we know that they are good for us—they help us learn to be patient. And patience develops strength of character in us and helps us trust God more each time we use it until finally

27

our hope and faith are strong and steady. Then, when that happens, we are able to hold our heads high no matter what happens and know that all is well, for we know how dearly God loves us, and we feel this warm love everywhere within us because God has given us the Holy Spirit to fill our hearts with His love (Rom. 5:3–5 LB).

LIFE'S TUNNELS

Many years ago, I heard someone say, "You live through the darkness from what you learned in the light." I am sure each person reading this book will be called on from time to time to walk through a dark tunnel. We will face heartaches and tears; we will pass through shadows of sickness, loneliness, separation, and death. "I have told you these things, so that in me you may have peace. In this world you will have trouble. But take heart! I have overcome the world" (John 16:33).

Jesus also suffered during His time on earth. But He taught us how to live through the suffering. He taught us that the faith we build by praying and reading and studying His Word will get us safely through the dark tunnels. He taught us to be confident, even in the midst of the tunnel, that He is with us and will lead us through. I like the word "through" because it has a starting point and an exit. Sometimes when we are in the midst of a grievous situation, we can't see the end of the tunnel; but it is there. And our strength comes from knowing that our Great Shepherd is going through the tunnel *with us* and that He will lead us out once again into the path of His golden sunlight. "Even though I walk *through* the valley of the shadow of death, I will fear no evil, for you are with me; your rod and your staff, they comfort me" (Ps. 23:4). Whether we ever see an angel or not, we can be absolutely certain of God's unlimited love for us.

I asked Jesus,
"How much do you love me?"

And Jesus said,
"This much . . ."
And He stretched out His arms
And died.

(unknown)

THE SCARS OF GRIEF

I remember one Christmas, not long ago, when our family was all together. We sat around the tree and began to reminisce about some happy memories. Our son Dan looked down at one of the scars on his hand and said, "I remember when I got this scar. We lived in Switzerland, and one day as I was walking down the road I fell on the ice and nearly cut my finger off with my new Swiss knife. Remember, Tom, how you and Franky Schaeffer helped me get to the nearest chalet? The artist who lived there invited us in and bound up my finger and gave us hot chocolate and cookies. Later he invited the whole family to his art show at the Palace Hotel in Villars."

The memories from that scar story led us to share other happy events. Each of us began to point out the scars we had accumulated over the years and to relate each story behind them. What an evening that was! Some scars had happy memories; others brought painful memories to mind. Some had healed over so you could hardly see them; others were still very tender, even though many years had gone by.

Every hurtful and unhappy experience we have leaves some kind of blemish on our life. At first some wounds are so severe they leave a deep, jagged, purple scar. Yet, if we don't keep digging at the sore spot, the tissues will knit together again and heal. Someday we will be able to look back and see that only a pale scar gives evidence of that painful ordeal. It may be tender to touch at times, but the wound has healed.

This is what happens when we meet with the disasters of life. As time passes, we notice the pain is no longer all-consuming. The injury has healed and only a scar remains. Once again, we are able to reach out to others. We start to live again. We realize we are able to share, in small ways at first, our love and concern for those nearest to us. We detect a renewed desire to serve the Lord Jesus whom we love and who never stopped loving us. When we get to heaven, I don't believe God is going to look for all the bright shining medals people have given to us here on earth; I believe He is going to look for the scars we accumulated during our lifetime. He's going to note how we got them and how well we let them heal.

Some of us may long for an angel experience, but Jesus often has something better for us. We want to mount up with wings like the eagles. We want to remain on the mountaintop of life and see the next extraordinary event from God. We want to be wrapped in the warm security blanket of God's protection and be kept from all harm. We have forgotten that Jesus has chosen instead to wrap us in the spotless robes of His righteousness here in the middle of a suffering world. C. G. Trumbull said, "Those who are readiest to trust God without evidence other than His Word, always receive the greatest number of visible evidences of His love."

And should we ever have a visible expression of the vast host of the heavenly angels that surround us, it will be even dearer to us because we have learned to trust Him without it. We have learned from experience that He alone is worthy of our confidence.

TRUST

As we walk close to Jesus each day, we learn to put our confidence in Him. We learn that the Christian life is not a series of supernatural interventions. Even if we have an angel experience, we do not expect them to become a nightly occurrence, as some popular books would have us believe. As our trust in God increases, we are prepared for the times of crisis that occasionally occur. We discover a firm foundation has been laid in our life. We become like the wise man who built his house on the rock. When the storms came, his house stood firm. But the house built on the sand by the foolish man, collapsed during the storm. The same rain fell on both houses, but it was the one whose foundation was built on the solid rock that stood firm.

To trust in God while the storms of life are raging all around us is a demonstration of the power of God in us. To continue our work in the middle of a disastrous situation, is evidence of the Holy Spirit working in us. God calls us to walk with Him and to trust Him each step of the way. We can be confident that when we walk through the hard, rocky places of life, God will give us protection for our journey.

> I cannot do it alone,
> The waves run fast and high,
> And the fog closes all around,
> The light goes out of the sky:
> But I know that we two
> Shall win in the end.
> Jesus and I.
> (unknown)

We may not experience the supernatural deliverance of an angel, but God promises us supernatural strength of spirit. Our faith and trust are made stronger and our character is strengthened when we pass through storms without the help of angels. We learn what Jesus meant when He said, ". . . blessed are those who have not seen and yet have believed" (John 20:29). We learn to trust God and His Word more than we trust an experience. Our strength always comes from knowing Jesus. ". . . I know whom I have believed, and am convinced that he is able to guard what I have entrusted to him. . . ." (2 Tim. 1:12).

Remember, the object of faith is what is important. And the object of our faith is Jesus Christ. Are we going to trust and love God more if we see an angel tonight? No. We love Him even if we never see an angel. God wants us to love Him for who He is, not because we have received signs and wonders.

ABOUT THE FOLLOWING STORIES

During the past few years, I have met people from all over the world who have taken the time to tell me their angel stories. It has been a special joy to listen to them tell their true experiences. Some of the names and places have been changed, but the contents of each story remain unchanged.

The purpose of this book is not to try to convince the skeptic of the supernatural world which surrounds us; it is simply to share with you some of the stories that were related to me by people I respect. My prayer is that each reader will become more aware of the fact that God sends His angels to minister to us in countless different ways. With this knowledge, we gain a new insight into the great, all-powerful, supernatural God of the Bible.

One thing that impressed me as I interviewed these people was the gentle way in which the angel made its presence known and the total absence of anything spectacular or sensational. I didn't find anyone who had an angel story who went around broadcasting it, who got up on a soapbox and proclaimed the experience, or who even tried to convince another person it was true. In fact, most were very reluctant to share the experience at all. In all cases, the memory of it has remained close to their hearts and often has been a source of comfort to them in other times of crisis. I never sensed that anyone felt spiritually superior as a result of having an angel experience. I found no semblance of any self-righteous attitudes. On the contrary, those who had had encounters with angels usually felt extremely humble. All were left with a serene reverence and a feeling of quiet wonder. There was never a doubt in any of their minds what had happened. They knew the presence was real, whether it was seen or unseen.

I am confident that, as you read the following stories, you will be encouraged by the magnificent truth that God sends His angels to minister to "those who will inherit Salvation" (Heb. 1:14). These stories will comfort you and your faith will be increased as you catch a glimpse of the glory of heaven and of the host of God's angels standing by, ready to help you at God's command. Joy and confidence will spring up in your heart as you realize that the ultimate supernatural event will be our resurrection to everlasting life with Christ in a place where there will be no more tears, pain, nor tragedy.

See His glory before you! Hear the songs of praises being sung! Hear the great choirs of angels as they sing: "To him who sits on the throne and to the Lamb be praise and honor and glory and power, for ever and ever!" (Rev. 5:13).

Part 2

THE
STORIES

For He will command His angels concerning you to guard you in all your ways; they will lift you up in their hands, so that you will not strike your foot against a stone.

Ps. 91:11, 12

IT WAS A HOT, humid summer day in the Midwest. Brian stopped by his friend's house to go swimming with some of his school friends. They spent the morning swimming and diving and having fun together. It was good to see the old gang again and Brian left reluctantly to do his summer job of mowing lawns.

That night he had a date with a girl who lived in the next town. As Brian drove home at the end of the evening, he noticed that the stars and moon had disappeared and that an eerie stillness filled the air. The hot summer night seemed to have cast a spell over the entire countryside. Everything was quiet and dripping with darkness. Before going home he decided to stop by his friend's house for a quick dip in the pool. It was late when he arrived, and the house was dark. Everyone was in bed. As he tiptoed quietly through the back yard, he imagined how good the cool water would feel as it passed over his body.

Brian climbed up on the diving board and stood poised, ready to dive into the pool. As he looked into the midnight blackness beneath him, he saw a very strange sight. There was a gleaming, brilliant glow in the shape of a cross. When he looked closer, he saw what seemed to be a glimmering angel stretched out in the darkness below. With eyes fastened on the silvery object, he slowly climbed down the ladder of the diving board. He walked to the edge of the pool and knelt down for a closer look. Instantly the glory was gone. And Brian found himself looking into a swimming pool without a drop of water in it! The next day he discovered that his friend's parents had drained the pool after they had finished swimming that morning in order to clean it.

This experience happened several years ago and Brian is now a senior in college. But there is a singing deep down in his heart every time he remembers that summer night and the angel who saved his life.

A YOUNG MOTHER was standing at the kitchen sink washing dishes one spring morning. Their little garden was aflame with fresh jewel-like flowers, and the smell of warm clover filled the air. In a moment of time, the long, dreary winter was forgotten.

As she looked out the window into the back yard, she noticed that the garden gate had been left open. Her little three-year-old daughter, Lisa, had toddled through the gate and was sitting casually on the railroad tracks playing with the gravel. The mother's heart stopped when she saw a train coming around the bend and heard its whistle blaring persistently. As she raced from the house screaming her daughter's name, she suddenly saw a striking figure, clothed in pure white, lifting Lisa off the tracks. While the train roared past, this glorious being stood by the track with an arm around the child. Together, they watched the train go by. When the mother reached her daughter's side, Lisa was standing alone.

JACKIE IS A BEAUTIFUL GIRL of seventeen years. She has shining black hair and sparkling brown eyes. A delightful glow sets her apart from other beautiful young girls. I first met her when I was speaking at the annual daffodil luncheon. She was one of the daffodil princesses. Dressed in a long yellow gown, she looked every bit as lovely as the spring flower she represented.

Three years ago, Jackie faced a painful tragedy. Doctors had discovered a tumor on her cheekbone—the kind of tumor usually found only on a long bone such as an arm or a leg. It had spread its deadly tentacles throughout the entire cheek region of her attractive face. Surgery offered the only hope to save Jackie's life. The doctors explained carefully to her and her parents exactly what the operation would include. They would be making an incision along the nose area and down through the upper lip. All of her teeth on the left side of her face would have to be removed as well as the cheekbone, the nose bone, and the jaw bone. Needless to say, an operation of this immensity, performed on the face of a lovely 14-year-old girl, was a grim prospect. Many tears were shed.

With deep sorrow Jackie packed her suitcase and set out for the hospital. Several days before surgery, lying in her hospital bed, she thought about what it would mean to go through life so terribly scarred, if indeed she even lived through the operation. She was frightened. She desperately wanted to live. She wanted to experience all that life held for her. As she tossed on her pillow in lonely fear that night, she began to pray. With tears of anxious apprehension, she asked God to help her.

About two o'clock in the morning, Jackie was awakened. She didn't know what woke her up; she only knew she was awake and alert. She saw a glowing light at the foot of her bed, and the silvery form of an angel appeared. The presence was very powerful, yet totally loving. An aura of stillness filled Jackie like the warmth of a summer day. She felt enfolded by the presence and a sense of incredible wonder touched every part of her body.

A voice filled with sunshine said, "Do not be afraid Jackie. You are going to be all right."

And then the angel was gone, leaving behind a radiance of pure loveliness.

The following day, Jackie was taken to the x-ray room for preoperative x-rays. To the utter astonishment of the doctors, every trace of the tumor and its deadly tentacles was gone.

That was three years ago. Now here she was, this beautiful daffodil princess, sitting next to me at the table. Her lovely face is unmarred, and she remains very much aware of God's miraculous touch upon her life.

THE WEEK HAD BEEN full and busy for the doctor. As he drove into his driveway that Saturday afternoon, he looked forward to putting on his old clothes, relaxing in front of the TV, and watching his favorite Buckeyes beat the Wolverines. Halfway through the game, the phone rang. There was an emergency at the hospital and he was needed immediately. He grabbed his bag and dashed out the door to his car in the driveway. He climbed in, turned on the key, and was ready to go. Suddenly he felt a strong presence standing by his open window. It was so real he felt he could reach out and touch it. He even paused long enough to turn his head and look. Although he didn't see anything, he heard a word of warning. "Don't back out of the driveway. Get out and look behind you."

Even though the doctor was in a tremendous hurry, he felt he must obey the message. He got out of his car, walked around to the back, and there he saw the little two-year-old boy from next door. He was sitting in his new rocking chair, leaning up against the back bumper of the doctor's car, watching the lazy autumn clouds float by.

KAREN HAD MIRACULOUSLY lived through a recent horrifying experience. She had been thrown into a car at gun point, taken out of town to a deserted woods, and raped. Before her attacker left, he shot her three times. Several hours passed before she was able to struggle to her feet. Unable to find her shoes, she stumbled barefoot out to the little-traveled highway. She knew she was a long way from town and would have to walk the entire way on the gravel road. Many times she felt certain she would never make it. She prayed and asked God to send someone to help her. In her weakness and near delirium, she suddenly felt as though she were being carried in strong protective arms. As she finally reached the edge of town, it seemed she was placed gently on the ground.

She saw a warm light shining from the window of the first house she came to, so she walked up on the porch and knocked on the door. A friendly young woman answered. She took one look at Karen and quietly slumped to the floor. Her husband rushed over to help Karen inside. He carefully led her to the couch and phoned for an ambulance. Then he went to help his wife who was just reviving.

Karen smiled weakly at her and said, "I'm sorry I frightened you. I know I look terrible."

But the young wife said, "No, that's not why I fainted. I saw a great shining angel holding you up as you stood at the door."

Later in the hospital, though Karen had walked barefoot several miles on a gravel road, not even a scratch could be found on her feet.

Surely the angel had carried her in its arms, "lest she dash her foot against the stone."

LINDA AND HER HUSBAND had been painting the outside of the house together. Since it was a warm, sunny afternoon and since the children were in bed taking a nap, she thought it would be a nice surprise if she could finish painting the trim around the upstairs windows before her husband arrived home from work.

She got out the tall ladder and climbed to the top. There wasn't any place to set the can of paint, so she had to hold it with one hand and paint with the other. She felt a little nervous up there so high above the ground. When she looked down, she noticed that the cyclone fence surrounding their property had a very sharp, jagged top. She thought to herself how terrible it would be if she fell and landed on top of those spikes.

As she continued painting, the ladder suddenly tipped backward and crashed to the ground. When Linda started to fall, she called out one word, "Jesus!"

The next thing she knew, she was standing quietly on the ground, still holding the can of paint in her hand—not one drop had spilled out. The ladder lay broken on top of the cyclone fence. Linda is sure that, in that brief instant, Jesus heard her frantic cry for help and sent an angel to set her gently on the ground.

EMILY GREW UP in a lovely southern town filled with charm. She was seven years old and it was her responsibility to walk home from school with her little five-year-old brother. Each day as they walked down the tree-shaded street, Emily looked forward to passing her favorite house. It was a large brick home set in a garden carpeted with flowers and surrounded by a tall iron fence. Emily always liked to imagine that it was the big old house where Beth and Jo lived from her favorite story, *Little Women*.

One afternoon as they were walking past the big house, she and her brother suddenly felt a hand on their shoulders. In an instant, they were picked up and placed gently down about fifteen feet away. In that same moment, a car came down the street at tremendous speed and ran up over the curb, smashing into the iron fence at the exact spot where Emily and her little brother had been walking. Had they been there, they would have been crushed into the fence. When Emily turned around to see who had picked them up, no one was there.

In the sixth month God sent the angel Gabriel to Nazareth, a town in Galilee, to a virgin pledged to be married to a man named Joseph, a descendant of David. The virgin's name was Mary. The angel went to her and said, "Greetings, you who are highly favored! The Lord is with you."

Mary was greatly troubled at his words and wondered what kind of greeting this might be. But the angel said to her, "Do not be afraid, Mary, you have found favor with God. You will be with child and give birth to a son, and you are to give him the name Jesus. He will be great and will be called the Son of the Most High. The Lord God will give him the throne of his father David, and he will reign over the house of Jacob forever; his kingdom will never end."

"How will this be," Mary asked the angel, "since I am a virgin?"

The angel answered, "The Holy Spirit will come upon you, and the power of the Most High will overshadow you. So the holy one to be born will be called the Son of God. Even Elizabeth your relative is going to have a child in her old age, and she who was said to be barren is in her sixth month. For nothing is impossible with God."

"I am the Lord's servant," Mary answered. "May it be to me as you have said." Then the angel left her.

Luke 1:26–38

The following three stories were chosen from several I collected that are similar. In each incident, the person sharing the story felt a strong hand on his/her shoulder and heard a specific message. First, I will share my story with you.

In 1962, MY HUSBAND and I and our three children had the privilege of spending six months in Switzerland, studying with Dr. Francis Schaeffer of L'Abri Fellowship.

Edith Schaeffer and I became good friends during those six months. Every Monday afternoon we drove down to the neighboring village to buy the week's supply of groceries for our households. Afterward, we always rewarded ourselves by stopping in a cozy tea room for a cream-chestnut tart and a cup of hot tea.

One Monday in early November as we sipped our tea Edith said, "Hope, be sure and save any Christmas money you get for the big winter sale that comes to all the stores in Switzerland during January." She went on to explain how Switzerland was different from the States, where there are sales almost continually. In Switzerland they only hold two sales a year. One is in January and the other is in late summer. All the stores participate.

From that day on, every extra penny we could save went into a special envelope marked "Winter Sale."

Finally the big week arrived. Edith said we should go on the first day of the sale and get there when the stores opened. As I counted the money in our special envelope, I found we had saved a little over $150.00. That was quite a sum back in 1962 and both Harry and I were pleased with our accomplishment. The night before the sale I carefully measured our children so I could adjust to the Swiss sizes. With the measurements and money tucked securely in my purse, Edith and I wound our way down the mountain road to Lausanne. There was an air of adventure in the car. We would not be home until after dinner.

We started our shopping in her favorite store and I did

something I have never done in my entire life. I found everything on my shopping list in the first store! I found two well-made jackets for the boys, with heavy lining to keep them warm in our cold Pittsburgh winters. For Debbie I found a pretty powder blue coat with colorful, embroidered flowers all around the yoke. It came with matching leggings and hat. I could just picture how adorable she would look next winter with her big brown eyes and rosey cheeks, wearing her pretty blue coat from Switzerland. For Harry I found a beautiful chocolate brown coat with soft lining and a warm jacket to wear to football games. For myself I chose an attractive blue woolen coat, trimmed with black braid around the collar, cuffs, and down the front. There was enough money left to buy all of us warm scarfs with matching hats and gloves.

As I carried my carefully chosen purchases to the cashier, I was filled with happiness. How fun it was to buy such nice Swiss clothes for my family! As the saleswoman began to ring up all the items, I suddenly felt a very strong hand on my shoulder. I turned around to see who it was, but no one was there. Yet there was no mistaking the solid pressure on my shoulder or the firm voice that accompanied it. A message was clearly communicated to me, "You won't be needing those things."

Since the strong hand was still on my shoulder, I turned again and said, "Of course I will need them. We live in Pittsburgh and it's cold there. Look, I got all bigger sizes for next year!" Who was I arguing with? I didn't know.

The message came once more, clear and unmistakable. "You won't be needing those things."

Then the hand was gone, the voice was gone, and the saleswoman was looking at me expectantly, obviously repeating the total price. "That will be $146.00, please."

I could hardly believe my own ears when I heard myself saying, "I'm sorry. I won't be needing these things." And I scooped them all up and returned them to their proper places on the rack. The rest of the day, Edith and I shopped together. We visited many stores and saw great bargains, but I didn't buy anything. When I walked into our little chalet at eight-thirty that night, Harry and the children were waiting with anticipation to see what I had bought. Can you imagine their dismayed surprise when I laid on the table the extent of my purchases—eighty-seven cents worth of peanuts and one pair of stockings!

Three weeks after we returned to Pittsburgh, however, I learned that the angel with the strong hand and firm voice had been right. The head of our mission telephoned and asked if we would pray about taking our family to Brazil in September and living there for the next five years to start the mission work there! Of course we went. And of course, we did not need the stack of beautiful Swiss winter clothes in Brazil.

MARY IS A KIND, loving woman who is often referred to by friends as a "saint in the Lord." She is the mother of nine children, with whom she lives in a Midwestern home filled with warmth and the love of God. Family prayer and Bible reading are given high priority, as well as church and Sunday school attendance.

Each year, the Fourth of July is celebrated with a parade in Mary's town. Many of the townspeople and local shop owners design colorful floats to enter in the parade. Much thought and preparation go into each one. The children love to sit expectantly on the curb and watch the gaily decorated floats go by, trailing their long streamers of crepe paper behind! Many of the children look forward to the day when they will be old enough to build a float to be entered in the big Fourth of July parade.

Bill, Mary's nineteen-year-old son and the eldest of her children, was one who had looked forward to building his own float. During the past winter he and his cousin had spent many nights designing and building a float to enter in the parade.

At last the day arrived. While it was still dark, Bill and his cousin went down to the fairgrounds where all the floats were lined up in order of appearance. They wanted to make sure everything was all right. Soon the streets were filled with thousands of people. Excitement was in the air. Fathers held small children up on their shoulders so they would not miss anything. Red, white, and blue balloons were tied securely to chubby fingers as little ones sat on the curb waiting for the magic moment. Picnic hampers, packed with every variety of delicious food and homemade pies, were setting on bright, red checkered tablecloths in the nearby park. Bill and his cousin were number eight in the parade lineup. As they sat waiting inside their float, the engine suddenly sounded as if it had a miss in it. They crawled up to the front and discovered some kind of mechanical difficulty had developed. Without warning, the

50

motor exploded and the entire float burst into flames. Bill was able to escape, but when he got outside he realized with horror that his cousin was still inside. He dashed back through a wall of smoke and was able to drag his cousin to safety. In the process, Bill caught on fire and was severely burned. An ambulance rushed him to the small hospital, but he died the following day.

The entire town mourned the loss of Bill. He had always been a good boy and was loved by everyone. His family was grief-stricken, and the children couldn't understand why this had happened to their big brother.

One day in mid-September when all the children were back in school and the house was quiet, Mary picked up her well-worn Bible and took it out to the sunny front porch. Her heart was still raw and desperately aching with grief. She had not had a moment's peace of mind since the day of the fire.

For seemingly the hundredth time, she cried out to God in despair, "Why? Why my Bill, Lord? He was such a good boy." And, as usually happened after this heart-wrenching cry, she broke into uncontrollable sobs. As the tears rained down on the worn pages of her open Bible, she suddenly felt a strong hand on her shoulder. A powerful presence of authority and total love was standing beside her. It was such a firm hand that she immediately stopped crying. She knew this was a holy moment and she was almost afraid to take a breath.

Then a crystal clear voice broke through the silence. "Mary, fear not. Your son is all right. He is with Jesus this very moment."

For the first time in months, a ray of warm sunshine began to creep into the cold corners of her grief-stricken heart. A peace and quietness replaced the aching despair. She felt a seed of love take root in the parched soil of her heart, and from that seed came a newness of life.

This story happened several years ago. The throbbing,

51

open wound of loss has healed, and only a tender scar remains in its place. Mary is learning that there usually is not an answer to the despairing, negative question, "Why, Lord?" Yet God does have an answer to the positive, life-renewing question, "How?" She is learning to ask, "Lord, *how* can I use this tragedy in my life for your glory? *How* can I use it to bring comfort and encouragement to others?" And this has made the difference. She is learning that God meets us in each loss and tragedy of life—He binds up the brokenhearted and comforts us with His love, just as He promised. And whenever a new wave of grief occasionally threatens to gather momentum and crash down around her, she is reminded of that day on her sunny porch when a supernatural hand of strength was laid on her shoulder, bringing a message of God's love, comfort, and healing.

DURING WORLD WAR II, George was a navigator on a B-24 bomber called The Liberator and was stationed in Italy. On one particular mission, his plane was flying over central Europe. As they approached the target area to be bombed, he felt a strong hand on his shoulder and heard a voice say to him, "Get up and go to the back of the plane."

In the brief moments that he was back there, a limited antiaircraft firing took place over the target area. When George returned to the front of the plane, he noticed a shell three inches in diameter had blown a hole in the ceiling of the plane and right through his navigator's seat.

To this day, he is confident God sent an angel to tell him to go to the back of the plane at that specific moment. He has remained conscious of God's hand on his life through the years and it has greatly added to his faith and trust in Him.

LAURA HOPED THE EVENTS of this particular day would never be repeated. Her teenage grandson, along with several friends, had gotten into serious trouble. The police car, with its siren blaring, had come down the quiet street and pulled into her daughter's driveway. All the neighbors seemed to rush to their windows to see what had happened. After the policemen left, taking Laura's grandson with them, everyone in the house was upset and sad. The mother and father were deeply concerned about their son. He had never given them any trouble before. What had happened? Maybe they should move away from their lovely home and start a new life. It would give him an opportunity to go to a different school and make new friends. Many tears were shed before the last light was turned out that night.

When Laura finally went to her room, her heart aching, she knelt down to pray for her family. A few hours after she had climbed wearily into bed and fallen asleep, she was awakened with a start. An intense light filled the room and a gloriously shining being was sitting at the foot of her bed. For some reason, however, she was not afraid. She heard a voice like the quiet song of a nightingale say, "God loves your grandson. Be calm and do not worry. You are to demonstrate God's love to him." And then the light was gone, but the glory remained.

She followed the angel's instructions and found many ways to show God's love to her grandson. As it turned out, that was the only time he ever got into trouble. In the years that followed, Laura and her grandson established a loving, loyal relationship between them. She regards this as one of her most cherished gifts in life.

KARL WAS SERIOUSLY ILL. He had long been battling a disease which plagued both kidneys. At last the doctor said his only hope was surgery. After the operation was completed, Karl was placed in the Intensive Care Unit for several days. At one point, his life literally hung in the balance. The doctor could give his family no assurance that he would live. He was burning with fever, and an infection had set in. At times, Karl wondered if he would ever see another day.

One afternoon when all hope seemed gone, a brilliant light, full of warmth and glory, filled Karl's corner of the Intensive Care Unit. He became conscious of a tall, majestic angel standing by his bed, radiating a source of immense strength and gentleness.

The angel smiled and said in a plain, clear voice, "Karl, you will be all right." Then the striking figure was gone.

Karl felt like he was covered with a featherweight blanket of healing energy. He knew he would get well.

Today he is a successful businessman who never forgets the angel God sent to him with the message of healing and hope.

EVELYN HAD BEEN a widow many years. After her children were grown and settled in homes of their own, God gave her a wonderful husband. Joe was a doctor who had lost his first wife ten years earlier. They had much in common and spent many happy years together. They built a lovely home overlooking the ocean and both enjoyed working in their garden. Joyous times were spent traveling and they were both grateful to God for bringing them together.

One day Joe had a serious heart attack, and the doctor said he would have to slow down. After four years of partial rest, however, tests showed he needed heart surgery. The doctor warned the couple that he was not sure Joe was strong enough to survive the operation. The decision had to be made by the husband and wife.

After going to sleep that night, Evelyn awoke, aware of a strong presence standing beside their bed. For an instant the room became a glow—every part of it was flooded by an all-encompassing light, accompanied by a feeling of enormous gladness. She remembers thinking "this must be a glimpse of what heaven is like." She knew it was an angel standing by the bed and was not surprised when the angel spoke to her.

"Your husband is stronger than you think," it said. "He is God's child. Do not fear."

Full of wonder, she woke her husband and told him what had happened. After talking it over in great detail, they said a prayer of thanksgiving. When they finished praying, they were too excited to go back to sleep. They sensed the presence of the angel still with them. An awesome quiet filled the room. Then the angel was gone, and the room was still and peaceful. They both dropped into a deep sleep.

A week later, tests showed the damaged artery had been closed off and a bypass had occurred naturally. They had many more wonderful years together.

See that you do not look down on one of these little ones. For I tell you that their angels in heaven always see the face of my Father in heaven.

Matt. 18:10

JOHN WAS A YOUNG BOY who lived in a big old farm house with his mother and father and five younger brothers and sisters in North Dakota.

One day John's parents went to another town on business and had to stay overnight. They left John in charge of the family. After the children had eaten dinner, they went upstairs to get ready for bed. All the brothers and sisters were gathered together in one bedroom. Suddenly John looked over at his two-year-old brother and saw, to his horror, that he was playing with a lighted candle. He was sticking unlit matches into it and watching with glee as they burst into flame. Before John could rush to his brother's side, the candle tipped over and fire began to spread. No one can explain why, but in the middle of all this the children looked over to the door. There they saw a tall, beautiful angel standing in the doorway. The angel simply blew out the fire and turned around and left. All the children ran down the hall after it, but the angel was gone.

Now the brothers and sisters are married and have children of their own. But when they get together, they often talk about the time they saw the angel blow out the fire that cold winter night.

GRETCHEN'S HUSBAND was the presiding judge of the Juvenile Court in Denver, Colorado. A brilliant and compassionate man, he believed that justice delayed was justice denied. This was especially true, he felt, when dealing with children. He often became deeply involved with the young people brought before his bench, and found himself working long hours to help them. One day he came home from work especially tired. He seemed to be coming down with the flu. A few days later his lungs filled up, and because he did not have the necessary resources left in his tired body to fight it, he died. It was a devastating blow to Gretchen and the three children. Family and loved ones came from near and far to attend the funeral. The church was crowded, and people were standing in the lobby and out on the front lawn. The governor of Colorado and all the people the judge had worked with came to pay their respects. But perhaps one of the greatest tributes to his life were the many young people who attended the service. They were the ones he had helped to put back on the right pathway of life during his years as judge.

Through all the heart-breaking months of adjustment that followed, Gretchen had one constant concern. How would she bring up her children without their father's strong hand of love and leadership? The two girls were about to enter junior high school. She understood the temptations that awaited them in this day of reckless permissiveness. Her six-year-old son was still a bundle of impish joy, but she knew from experience with her husband's work the pitfalls that lay before him. How could she possibly raise these three children alone in today's world?

One Sunday late in September, Gretchen and her children were walking home from church. It was a sunny Colorado day. The air was crisp and clear. The peaks of the majestic Rocky Mountains pierced the brilliant blue of a cloudless sky. The fragrance of late-blooming flowers filled the air with the sweet breath of autumn. Gretchen decided this would be a good day to take pictures of the children for Christmas cards to be sent later that year. A quick brushing of their hair and everything was ready. She placed her two daughters on either side of her son. A lump caught in her throat as she looked at these three beautiful children. How precious they were to her, and how vulnerable to the hurts and disappointments of life.

A few weeks later, Gretchen picked up the developed pictures. They all turned out good. In fact, it was difficult to select one for the Christmas cards. But wait, what was this? On one of the pictures, a tall majestic form appeared to be standing behind the children. Its arms were outstretched as though it was protecting them. Gretchen quickly shuffled through the pictures again to see if this form was on any of the others. It wasn't. What could it be? Could it possibly be an angel? She took the pictures back to the camera shop and showed them to the man who had developed them. No one could explain the form. It was clearly visible on the negative as well. When she showed the picture to her rector at church, he smiled happily and said, "Now you have a picture of your children's guardian angel."

From that day on, Gretchen knew she would not have to raise her children alone. Her fear and concern were replaced with a peace and confidence in God. She knew He would give her the necessary wisdom and love to bring them up properly. Her strength came from the certainty that God's shield of protection surrounded them and that He would guard them from evil and harm. This has proven true. Her family has been greatly blessed. Both girls are now in college and her son is finishing junior high school. They face life with a twinkle in their eyes. They are learning to cope with the trials of life as well as with the joys of success. And most important of all, each one is strengthened by a personal faith in the living God. They know His hand of protection and love is guiding them through life.

ONE HOT SUMMER DAY in 1900 in the dirt-farming community of northern Georgia, four-year-old Ernest and his mother went out to gather the straw from their large broom-straw farm. As far as Ernest could see, there was acre after acre of broom-straw, growing high above his head. He and his mother worked side by side all morning.

Soon the sun began getting hotter and Ernest became very hungry. He looked up from his work to complain to his mother, but she wasn't there. He began to run up and down the aisles of broom-straw crying her name; but he couldn't find her any place. By now he was very frightened because he was lost and didn't know how to find his way out of the tall lanes of straw. He sat down on the dirt and began to cry. Suddenly he saw his mother. She was holding out her hand to him and saying in a gentle voice, "Come, let's go home."

When they arrived at the house, Ernest's worried mother was standing on the porch.

"Where have you been, son?" she asked.

Through his dried tears, Ernest replied, "I was lost until you came and got me."

"I didn't come and get you," his mother said in surprise. "I couldn't find you and thought you had wandered back to the house."

ONE CRISP AUTUMN DAY in New England, five-year-old Bobbie was playing with his ball. It rolled out into the street and right down inside a huge storm drain. He loved his big blue ball and didn't want to loose it, so he started to climb down into the sewer after it. But at the entrance, an enormous white angel was standing, blocking the way. It simply shook its head back and forth saying "no."

Today Bob is a successful businessman, but he remembers seeing his guardian angel as if it were yesterday.

The following story is special because it was told to my husband and me one day in Chicago when we were very discouraged. We had been asked by our mission to move from colorful Colorado to Illinois. In our search to find a decent house we could afford, God led us to Kirk, a successful Christian real estate man. After spending the morning house hunting, we were having lunch with him in a nice restaurant. He told us the following story. By the time he finished it, he had a big white handkerchief out, wiping the tears from his eyes. It is a lovely story of God's tender care for His little children.

K IRK WAS EIGHT YEARS OLD when the depression was at its peak. He had several younger brothers and sisters, and his father was barely able to keep enough food on the table. Kirk's chore each Saturday was to take his red wagon and the shopping list his mother prepared and to walk down to the corner store to do the weekly shopping. His mother always gave him ten dollars for the food. With money being so scarce, it was a trusted job and Kirk carried it out with a strong sense of responsibility.

One Saturday morning his mother tucked the ten dollars into his jacket pocket and sent him off with a stern warning not to buy anything except what was on the list. When Kirk filled his wagon with the necessary food, he went to pay the lady at the counter. But when he reached into his jacket pocket, he could not find the money! Frantically, he searched through every pocket. Then he took off his shoes and socks, thinking he might have put the money there for safety. He looked under his cap and every place he could think of, but no money was found. He was filled with panic and began to cry. There was nothing to do but leave his wagon of food at the store and go home and tell his mother the sad truth. She was very angry and upset and although she searched in every pocket several times, she could not find the money either.

Knowing that the family would not have much to eat the following week, Kirk went down into the basement and cried heartbrokenly. Through his sobs, he heard a strong, kind voice calling him by name. It was accompanied by a presence of total love.

"Kirk, look in your jacket pocket."

What a strange thing to say. He had already been through his pockets many times. So had the owner of the store and so had his mother. But he was obedient to the voice and looked in his jacket pocket. There he found the ten dollars.

No one knows how it got there. Kirk is over sixty years old today, but he remembers that story as one of the shining moments of his life. Whenever he gets discouraged, he remembers that day in the basement when God heard the cries of a desperate little boy and sent a messenger to put ten dollars into his jacket pocket.

ERIK WAS THREE YEARS OLD and was staying with his grandparents for a few days while his mother and father went on a vacation.

One morning he woke up complaining that his ears hurt. He had a fever and ached all over. The grandmother phoned the doctor but couldn't get an appointment until seven o'clock that evening. Erik was crying and wanted his grandmother to hold him. It looked like it was going to be a long day for both of them.

Later in the morning, grandmother put Erik down on the living room rug with some of his toys, hoping they would occupy him for a little while. Then she went into her bedroom to pray. She asked God to be with Erik and to send His angels to entertain him.

Later, when grandmother was in the kitchen, Erik came running in from the living room shouting, "Grandma! Grandma! Come and see the angels!" He told her there were five angels and they were dancing and that they were wearing green dresses!

No one had ever told Erik about angels before and whenever anyone questioned him about them after that, they could not get him to change his story. He *knew* what he had seen.

Later that evening when the doctor checked him over, he said Erik did have both ears infected but the pain was gone and there was no fever.

As JANET PASSED the baby's room on her way to bed, she stopped, as she did every night, to say a prayer for her sleeping child. When she walked into the bedroom, she clearly saw two beautiful angels clothed in pearly radiance, standing by the baby's crib. They seemed to exude an air of infectious joy and delightful serenity. The sight was so totally unexpected that she paused to take in this moment of wonder. When she walked toward the crib the angels vanished, but their intense presence of love and joy remained in the room.

EVA WAS A LITTLE five-year-old girl out playing in the sunny California poppy fields. Suddenly, in the middle of this canopy of flowers stood an angel of incomparable beauty. It wasn't like any angel she had seen in pictures or like anything she had ever imagined. There was a glowing brightness all around it like radiant beams of sunlight. It had the sweetest expression on its face, and the little girl knew instantly it must be her guardian angel. She had an unbearable longing to throw her arms around this beautiful being, but the angel reached out to Eva first and enfolded her in arms of love.

Eva hurried home to tell her mother about the beautiful shining angel she had seen in the meadow. But her mother was busy working and just nodded a hurried, "Yes, yes."

Crestfallen, Eva walked out the door and found her old German grandmother sitting on the front porch, rocking quietly in the warm sunshine. She climbed up on her lap and told her about the lovely experience she had had that morning. As Eva talked, tears streamed down the wrinkled face of her grandmother. She held Eva close and wanted to hear every single detail.

When Eva finished her breathless story of wonder, the grandmother said, "Eva, never ever forget this moment. We all have guardian angels, but not many people get to see theirs in their lifetime. Remember, your angel will always be with you."

How grateful Eva was for her grandmother's understanding and for her belief in her. She knew what her grandmother said was true and from that day on she was rarely afraid of the dark or afraid to be alone.

As she grew up, she faced many difficulties in life. There were times when she longed to see her angel again, but Eva found there was no way she could command it to appear. And she learned it was Jesus she had to turn to, not an angel. But the joy and wonder of that long-ago experience in the sunny poppy fields of California never left her.

ONE NIGHT SHARON was tucking her youngest son, Tommy, into bed. After she had read a story to him from his favorite book and had prayed with him, four-year-old Tommy was still restless and didn't want his mother to leave. He said he was afraid of the dark. Sharon assured him that God has guardian angels to protect His children. "In fact," she said, "there is probably one right here in the room with you now, ready to take care of you while you sleep."

After a few moments of silence, Tommy said with a troubled voice, "But Mommie, I want someone with skin on them!"

So Peter was kept in prison, but the church was earnestly praying to God for him.

The night before Herod was to bring him to trial, Peter was sleeping between two soldiers, bound with two chains, and sentries stood guard at the entrance. Suddenly an angel of the Lord appeared and a light shone in the cell. He struck Peter on the side and woke him up. "Quick, get up!" he said, and the chains fell off Peter's wrists.

Then the angel said to him, "Put on your clothes and sandals." And Peter did so. "Wrap your cloak around you and follow me," the angel told him. Peter followed him out of the prison, but he had no idea that what the angel was doing was really happening; he thought he was seeing a vision. They passed the first and second guards and came to the iron gate leading to the city. It opened for them by itself, and they went through it. When they had walked the length of one street, suddenly the angel left him.

Acts 12:5–10

LATVIA IS A picturesque country nestled between the Baltic Sea and Russia. It is a country of fragrant woods, singing streams, and sloping meadows covered with flowers. In 1940, Russia seized this patriotic country and made it into a communist state.

Rudolf was a young, dedicated school teacher who was proud of his Latvian country. One day in 1942 he was suddenly taken away from home and placed in the Daugavdils Concentration Camp for "political reasons." Life there was a grim and bleak existence of cold, black nights followed by senseless empty days. Weeks soon became months, and Rudolf yearned for the day when his cell door would open and he would be free again. During the long, interminable nights, he would often remember how the birds used to fill the countryside with their songs on summer mornings and the way the fresh clover smelled in the warm sunshine. Would the day ever come when he would be free to experience these simple joys again?

After he had been a prisoner for six months, all hope for his release seemed to be gone. One afternoon as he sat in his cell, he put his head in his hands and began to pray. "Is there any help, Lord? Is there any hope?"

Suddenly, a brilliant light flooded his cell and stood as a great wall of light before him. And although he had not seen the sunlight for over six months, this vivid light did not hurt his eyes. In the middle of the wall of white light there appeared this message: "23 September." It was written in bold black letters.

He heard a clear, steady voice say, "That's the date when you will be free. Do not tell anyone this date." The words sang their way into his heart with a renewed message of hope.

Then the cell began to dim as though the sun had slipped behind a cloud, and the light was gone. Rudolf was left once again in the cold darkness. Only there was a difference. Instead of bitter despair, a quiet warmth began to soak through to his lonely heart. A sense of peace surrounded him and he felt secure and loved by God. He knew that September 23 was still six weeks away, but a small seed of faith took root in his soul, giving him new courage and strength. He did not tell his cellmates about his coming release for fear one of them might be a spy.

At last the long awaited date arrived. If anyone was to be set free in that prison, it always took place at ten o'clock in the morning. However, ten o'clock came and went without the promised freedom. At two o'clock, (the same time he had seen the great light in his cell six weeks earlier) the door swung open and a guard's voice pierced the darkness. "Rudolf Matiss, pick up your belongings and come to the office!" With no explanation, he was given his passport with the words, "You are free to go!"

He walked away from that bleak concentration camp that afternoon with the autumn sunshine brushing his face and the soft wind filling him with the fresh breath of freedom.

For the past forty years, September 23 has remained a special day of celebration for Rudolf. He remembers it with a feeling of peace deep in his soul that has never left him.

IT WAS A BRILLIANT sunny day on the silver beach of Hawaii. The air was fragrant with the smell of salt and the freshness of the sea. The golden sunlight brushed the earth with warm rays of contentment. David worked with an organization called "Youth With a Mission." He and his family were spending a day at the beach. Later in the afternoon, his wife and children returned home; but David decided to stay longer and get some sleep. About three o'clock, the surf started to pick up and a strong undertow developed. The ocean became rough and dark, and the waves rose to a foreboding ten feet. People hurried out of the water as quickly as possible.

David was enjoying a restful sleep on the beach when suddenly he was awakened and was instantly alert. (He is not normally "instantly alert" when he wakes up!) Wondering why he was so wide awake, he looked toward the water and saw a young mother running frantically into the crashing waves. Out beyond the impact zone, David saw a tiny head bobbing up and down. He raced into the water to help. Since he was an expert body-surfer and had spent much time in the water, he knew exactly how to handle the waves and what to do. When he reached the young mother and her little girl, they were struggling helplessly. He had never seen a more terrified look than the one he saw in the eyes of the young mother. He grabbed the little girl and hollered that he would be right back for the mother. There was no way he could have handled both of them in those thundering waves and against the powerful undertow.

About this time, Ruth, who worked with the same mission group as David, went down by the water to check on her son who was playing in the sand.

A nearby swimmer pointed out the drowning woman to Ruth and said, "That lady needs help, but I can't swim."

With vigorous strokes, Ruth began to swim out toward the sinking mother. When she reached the lady, the combination of high waves and the pull of the undertow' made the mother too heavy for Ruth to help. After much struggling and gasping for air, it began to look as if both of them would go under. Just then a man in red swimming trunks suddenly appeared behind them. He seemed to come out of nowhere because seconds earlier no one was around. With strong arms, he picked the lady up and carried her to shore. He gently put her down on the sand and Ruth helped her the rest of the way up the beach. She turned around to thank the man for his help, but he was nowhere in sight. No one on the beach could find the man in the red swimming trunks.

Later, David and Ruth drove the lady and her little girl home. The mother thanked them again and again for saving their lives. She mentioned how strong and secure the arms were that picked her up and how safe she felt as the man brought her to shore. When they reached her house she went in to get a picture her little girl had drawn in Sunday school the previous Sunday. She wanted to show it to David and Ruth. It was a picture of a mother and child, drawn in blue crayon, standing on the beach. And there was a man in red swimming trunks with them, holding their hands. Last Sunday when the mother had asked her little girl who the people in the picture were, she had answered, "Why it's you and me, mommie, and the man in the red bathing suit is Jesus."

ONE SUMMER DAY Bo went out in a small boat with three friends. Suddenly a storm came up. The sky darkened and the wind became a gusty gale. Lightning streaked across the sky. The waves became higher and higher until finally their boat tipped over and the friends were separated from one another. Bo began swimming toward shore but he couldn't keep his head above the waves. He kept sinking and gasping for air. The harder he swam, the farther back he was tossed by the waves. The more he struggled, the more he sank. He was frantic and felt sure he would never make it.

Then, from out of nowhere, a scuba diver came and with arms as strong as granite, carried Bo to shore. When Bo turned around to thank him, no one was there. About fifty yards down the beach, Bo found his three friends, safe and sound. Only the boat was lost.

DIANE, A YOUNG Christian university student, was home for the summer. She had gone to visit friends one evening and the time passed quickly as each shared their various experiences of the past year. She ended up staying longer than she had planned and had to walk home alone. But she wasn't afraid because it was a small town and she lived only a few blocks away. As she walked along under the tall elm trees, Diane asked God to keep her from harm and danger. When she reached the alley, which was a short cut to her house, she decided to take it.

However, halfway down the alley she noticed a man standing at the end as though he were waiting for her. She became uneasy and shot up a prayer asking for God's protection. Instantly a comfortable feeling of quietness and security surrounded her. She had the unmistakable sense that someone was walking with her. When she reached the end of the alley, she walked right past the man and arrived home safely.

The following day she read in the paper that a young girl had been raped in the same alley, just twenty minutes after she had been there. Diane thought she could possibly recognize the man and went down to the police station where she told her story. They asked her if she would be willing to look at a lineup to see if she could identify him. She agreed and immediately pointed out the man she had seen in the alley the night before. She asked the policeman if he would ask the man one question for her. She was curious to know why he had not attacked her.

When the policeman asked him, the man answered, "Because she wasn't alone. She had two tall men walking on either side of her."

M<small>RS.</small> ENGHOLM LIVED with her husband in a small guest house on an avocado ranch in California. It looked out across a peaceful meadow, carpeted with wildflowers. One day her husband became very ill. Soon after, with the family by his side, he was ushered into the presence of the living God, whom he loved and served.

A few days after his death, Mrs. Engholm awoke with a dreadful feeling of restlessness. She had to get away by herself and thought maybe a drive in the country would help. As she climbed into her car, she had no special destination in mind. She only knew she could not bear to stay in the house a moment longer. The day was especially beautiful and sunny, and she soon found herself traveling an unknown road. After driving for sometime, she came to a lovely lagoon surrounded by blue mountains.

As she sat and watched the peaceful scene before her, she decided to walk through the warm meadow down to the edge of the water. There she found a sunny rock on which to sit and enjoy the beauty of God's creation. She wasn't praying, and she wasn't thinking of anything special. She was just sitting there, letting the fragrance of summer fill her hurting, sorrowful spirit. All at once it seemed as if heaven opened up just a crack and filled the air with a breathless wonder. She felt a warm, loving presence standing behind her.

This powerful being communicated a specific message to her concerning her back. She had suffered with osteoarthritis of the spine for many years. The discs had disintegrated and the pain caused by bone rubbing against bone was excruciating. The angelic being told her that a fusion was taking place in her back and that she would be stronger and that her back would be healed. When the heavenly presence was gone, she lingered by the peaceful lagoon for a long time, letting the quiet serenity of the moment sink deep into her heart.

At last, refreshed and renewed, she turned to walk

back to her car to drive home. Instead of the empty restlessness and sorrow of the morning, she now felt comforted and brimming over with a feeling of expectant hope.

Several months later, x-rays revealed that her back had fused together. One morning last week she awoke from her first pain-free night in years. Today there is a radiant joy in her heart as she remembers the promise of healing God sent to her through His messenger.

The next three stories tell of an unseen presence that reached out and protected a person during a serious fall.

JAN'S DREAM HAD come true. She had been chosen to be a guide for the rigorous "Beyond Malibu" stress camp, a part of the Young Life summer program in the snow-covered mountains above the spectacular Princess Louisa Inlet in British Columbia. During a break between camps, Jan and two other guides made a trip into the mountains to find a new trail. Once there, they split up and each went searching in a different direction. Ordinarily they would not have done this, but since they would all be within close proximity of one another they thought it would be all right.

The snow was deep, and the place where Jan was hiking was steep and slippery. Suddenly she lost her balance, forgot the importance of maintaining a three-point stance, and reached out with both hands for the branch of a bush. She missed it, fell down on her back with a sickening thud, and began to slide down the mountain. As she gathered momentum, she noticed with helpless horror that she was heading straight toward the edge of a steep precipice which dropped thousands of feet to the inlet below. There was no way she could stop—nothing to grab on to in the white maze that flew past her.

She cried out, "God, please don't let me die!"

Just as she reached the edge, she felt a strong presence in front of her. The powerful being stopped her forward motion and pushed her from the steep edge of the cliff to about fifteen feet away.

When the other two guides found her, they could see the place where Jan had fallen. The exact line of her fall was clearly marked in the snow. But at the very edge of the cliff the line turned sharply at a right angle and came to rest fifteen feet away, where Jan lay. She had broken her back in the fall, but within a few months she was well and praising the Lord for sending His angel to rescue her.

THE DAY JANIE and her family had been waiting for so long had finally arrived. Today they were moving into their newly completed home. The only unfinished part of the house was the large circular staircase in the middle of the entrance hall. The workmen had left a scaffold to use to finish their work. It went through the center of the stairs and stood about fourteen feet from the ground.

As the moving van drove off that day, Janie's good friend stopped by to see if she could help. She noticed the stairway without a railing and the high scaffolding. She drew Janie aside and asked if she could say a prayer of protection for the family until the stairway was completed. Janie was a fairly new Christian at the time and had never thought of praying about such a thing. But she agreed, and together they prayed for God's protection around that dangerous work area.

The next week, Janie's five-year-old daughter was playing superman. She had on her superman costume, complete with a big red "S" on the front. The high scaffolding seemed like a good place from which to make a "rescue." She walked fearlessly out to the middle of it, feeling very brave. When she looked down she suddenly became frightened, lost her balance, and fell from the scaffold.

Janie heard her daughter's frantic scream, "Mommie, help!" and turned around in time to see her little girl falling. Then suddenly, from out of nowhere, strong, invisible arms reached out and caught her, laying her carefully down on her back on the brick floor below.

Janie remembered the many stories she had heard of the importance of not moving a person after a serious fall or accident. She ran to call the emergency center. When the firemen and medics arrived, they could not believe that the little girl had not been hurt. She had no broken bones and not a sign of a scratch or a bruise.

During the years since that time, both Janie and her

daughter have grown closer to the Lord. They have memorized many of God's promises. But the promise that stands out forever in their minds is "He shall give His angels charge over you to guard you in all your ways."

JEANINE AND GREG had spent much time remodeling their little house to make it reflect their personalities and interests. One of the last things they did was remove the door that connected the kitchen to the living room to make an easier passageway between the two rooms. They had neglected, however, to remove the pointed hinges that jutted out from the door frame.

One quiet afternoon when their baby girl was learning to walk, Jeanine watched with loving amusement as she bravely took a few steps and then fell. With this trial and error method, the child was just about to walk through the door that led into the kitchen when she tripped on the metal stripping that held the carpeting down. Jeanine was sitting in the living room watching when the most interesting thing happened. As the baby lost her balance and began to fall, her eye was aimed right at the protruding bottom hinge. Jeanine tried to reach her before she hit her eye. But all at once, as she was falling forward, the baby bumped into something strong and invisible with so much force that she was pushed backward and landed instead on her well-padded bottom.

Jeanine ran over and hugged her baby tightly, confident that a guardian angel had reached out and protected her from injuring her eye.

"Thank you, Jesus," she whispered, "for sending your angels to care for these little ones."

I especially enjoyed the simple beauty of some of the stories shared with me. They are stories of God's constant awareness of every detail of our life—what we are doing and what we are experiencing at every instant. The following story is a demonstration of God's care even in little things.

MARGUERITE WAS AWAKENED in the middle of the night feeling sick. She didn't want to disturb her husband, so she quietly got out of bed and walked down the dark hall to the bathroom. She thought maybe an aspirin would help. As she stood over the bathroom sink, suddenly her head began to whirl and she started to fall. Her last thought was, "I'm going to hit my head on the edge of the sink!"

A few moments later Marguerite came to. Not only had she not hit her head on the sink, but to her utter amazement, she found she was neatly stretched out on her back, as though someone had gently laid her down. Even her nightgown was arranged neatly around her ankles. A feeling of peace, like the mist of a rainbow, surrounded her. This peace sang its way into her heart and filled every part of her being with music. As she walked back to bed, this peaceful presence went with her. She laid down and fell into a deep sleep. For several days this vibrant sense of quietness remained with her. This lovely experience from Marguerite's life is a moment she will cherish forever.

SHARON AND DOUG already had three dear children, ages fourteen, twelve, and ten; and Sharon, at age forty, was expecting the birth of their fourth child any day. The nine months of waiting had been a special time for the entire family. They looked forward to the arrival of the new baby with great anticipation.

Sharon and Doug liked to walk one or two miles each day. They usually walked holding hands and took their little gray terripoo dog with them on a leash. One afternoon they were walking down a hill near home when they momentarily dropped hands. Both of them were watching the dog run along side them with great excitement. Suddenly, Sharon turned her foot on a stone in the street and fell down. But instead of falling to the ground and rolling down the hill, she felt as though someone lifted her up and laid her down gently on the street. It was the most graceful, relaxed feeling she had ever experienced. When Doug turned to catch her, she was already stretched out full length beside his feet. The fall could have been extremely harmful to the expectant mother and unborn child. Yet a feeling of total quietness filled her and not one part of her or the baby was hurt.

Sharon believes her guardian angel laid her down ever so gently in the street that day, in special care for her and the new little life within her.

So the king gave the order, and they brought Daniel and threw him into the lions' den. The king said to Daniel, "May your God, whom you serve continually, rescue you!"

A stone was brought and placed over the mouth of the den, and the king sealed it with his own signet ring and with the rings of his nobles, so that Daniel's situation might not be changed. Then the king returned to his palace and spent the night without eating and without any entertainment being brought to him. And he could not sleep.

At the first light of dawn, the king got up and hurried to the lions' den. When he came near the den, he called to Daniel in an anguished voice, "Daniel, servant of the living God, has your God, whom you serve continually, been able to rescue you from the lions?"

Daniel answered, "O king, live forever! My God sent his angel, and he shut the mouths of the lions. They have not hurt me, because I was found innocent in his sight. Nor have I ever done any wrong before you, O king."

The king was overjoyed and gave orders to lift Daniel out of the den. And when Daniel was lifted from the den, no wound was found on him, because he had trusted in his God.

Dan. 6:16–23

ONE SNOWY WINTER NIGHT in a small Ohio town, nineteen-year-old Laurie was helping the librarian move all the books into the new church library. They had become so engrossed in their work that they forgot to notice the time. Soon it was after eleven o'clock. Laurie would have to run to catch the last bus home. She said good-bye to the other two girls who were helping and stepped out into the cold night air, drawing her coat around her and pulling the collar up over her ears to keep warm.

When she got on the bus she noticed she was the only passenger. Most people were home in their warm houses on this kind of a night. As the bus drove through the depressed area of town, it stopped to pick up a disheveled looking man. He looked Laurie over with a leering eye, sat down across the aisle from her, and attempted to make conversation. Laurie was frightened and prayed that he would get off the bus before they reached her stop, but he didn't.

At last the bus arrived at her corner, and she stood up to leave by the front door. To her dismay, she noticed that he was leaving by the back door. As the bus drove off and left her standing alone in the darkness, she sent up a frantic prayer for help. Then, to her utter amazement, as the man walked toward her she saw a beautiful white dog standing majestically at the bus stop as though he was waiting just for her. He was a Grand Pyrenees and must have weighed over two hundred pounds. As soon as she stepped off the bus, this tall, stately dog walked over to her and guarded her all the way home.

The man followed her for half a block and then turned and walked off in the opposite direction. The dog walked with Laurie right up to her front steps and then was gone.

The next day Laurie checked with all the neighbors to see who owned the beautiful dog, but no one did and Laurie never saw him again.

SUSAN WAS A LITTLE ten-year-old girl who lived in North Carolina and attended a Christian day school. There she learned how to pray and was daily nurtured in her faith in Jesus Christ. She came to believe that she truly was special in His sight.

One day when she was out in the front yard playing ball with her friends, the ball rolled across the street. Susan went running after it as fast as she could and didn't see the oncoming car. Suddenly she felt herself being lifted, held in midair, and placed gently on the other side of the street in a neighbor's yard. The auto screeched to a stop and the man and woman ran out to see if she was hurt. Everyone was stunned when they discovered she was totally unharmed. The couple told all the people who gathered on the lawn that they had seen Susan lifted into the air and over their car.

Although Susan is now a young married woman with children of her own, she has never forgotten that warm summer day when God sent a guardian angel to rescue her. The knowledge of this truth has been a tremendous source of spiritual blessing to her through the years.

DURING WORLD WAR II Marilyn's husband, Jim, was in the infantry in Germany. Those were difficult days for everyone around the world, but it was especially hard to be a young bride living daily in fear of getting one of those dreaded telegrams from the United States government.

Marilyn had a job at Lockheed Aircraft, working as a riveter inside the wings of large bombers. One morning as she was getting ready for work, the doorbell rang. No one came calling that early, so with a heart pounding with fear she went to the door. At the curb she saw an official government car, and standing on the porch was a man wearing an immaculate uniform. He had a sad yet kind face as he handed her a telegram. She tore it open and read the grim words, "We regret to inform you that your husband is reported missing in action." That was all. No mention of his whereabouts or how it had happened.

As the weeks dragged into months, Marilyn learned to live with fragmented emotions. Was her husband dead, or was he suffering the misery of prison camp? One night as she was on her knees praying for Jim, she began to cry in agony.

"Oh Lord," she sobbed, "it's so hard not knowing if my husband is dead or alive. If I could just have some definite word I really believe I could stand anything."

Instantly the room was filled with a vivid presence. Someone was standing behind her. She *knew* it—she felt it—and she was terrified. She started to turn around, but a voice pierced the silence.

"Do not be afraid, and do not turn around."

To her surprise, the fear dissolved and a quietness settled around her. She remained in the presence of this splendid being while waves of peace washed over her like a mist of silver spray.

Then a voice as clear as crystal said, "You will hear April 13." And then the angelic being was gone.

Two weeks later, on April 13, Marilyn received a post

card written in her husband's handwriting saying he was safe. He had been captured in the savage Battle of the Bulge, where hundreds of soldiers lost their lives, and was a prisoner of war in Germany. When the war was over, Jim returned home safely.

THE NARROW MOUNTAIN ROAD was full of hairpin curves. Jean and her family were on vacation driving through the great Rocky Mountain National Park in a convertible with no roll bars on the top. Fortunately, however, since it had been raining that morning, the top of the car was up.

All at once a large truck came around the bend from the opposite direction, heading straight for them! The truck's horn blew wildly, making the family think its brakes must have given out. Jean's husband turned the steering wheel sharply to his left to avoid a head-on collision. But he lost control of the car and it went off the road, turning over and over as it rolled down the mountainside. The car hit enormous boulders; but instead of being smashed to pieces, the car bounced from one boulder to another, as though they were soft clouds. Inside, the car was filled with an intense presence of peace. No one screamed. The occupants seemed to be wrapped in a blanket of protection, and the car seemed to be floating like a feather, rather than falling. Finally it came to rest, landing on the roof. The car was totally demolished, but not one member of the family had even a scratch.

THE HOSPITAL CORRIDOR was quiet. Visiting hours were over, and the last patient had been tucked in. Barbara was lying in bed, dangerously ill. Her friends had been taking turns sitting by her side for the past several days so she would not be alone. Each evening her husband arrived after dinner and sat with her through most of the night.

One evening the doctor came into the darkened room to check her before going home. When he finished he asked her husband to step out into the hall. Barbara heard the doctor say she could not last more than a day or two longer. There didn't seem to be any hope.

Later that night Barbara was awakened by a soft glowing light which permeated the room. She felt a presence cover her entire body—feet on feet, hands on hands, head on head—like a soft living blanket. She fell into a deep, peaceful sleep.

The following morning she awoke with a joy in her heart she couldn't explain. Then she remembered the presence of the night before and called the nurse to see if there was any change in her condition.

The next day Barbara left the hospital. That was twelve years ago, and she has never been sick since.

OCCASIONALLY SOUTH CAROLINA is hit by especially violent thunderstorms. Lillian's house is on a large corner lot and is prone to being struck by lightning. During most storms, the family goes downstairs and waits until it is over.

One day an exceptionally severe morning storm hit the area. The lightning streaked across the sky and the thunder exploded. Lillian thought it was the worst storm she had ever experienced. She ran upstairs to get her little girl to take her to the basement. But the child had been very sick during the night and had just fallen asleep, so Lillian decided it would be better to lie down beside her and pray that the storm would soon pass. Instead, however, the storm became more fierce as the lightning ripped through the air, snapping and crashing all around. A cold knot of fear gripped her heart, and she prayed for God's protection.

Instantly Lillian became aware of a presence of quietness in the middle of the violent storm. The quietness filled the room, and a hand of strength and authority touched her. Then it seemed she and her little girl were wrapped in unseen arms. She felt totally secure and wonderfully calm. The lightning struck in the hall, just on the other side of the wall from where they were lying; but neither of them was harmed.

Lillian is confident to this day that God sent an angel to hold them securely in arms of protection.

HEIDI'S MOTHER WAS a widow with several children to raise by herself. She worked long, strenuous hours to pay the living expenses and to keep the family together. After a hard day of working in the city, she would come home and wearily help prepare dinner and get the children settled down for the night. She often fell into bed exhausted but never went to sleep without first kneeling down by her bed to pray for the children.

When she came to Heidi's name while praying one night, she felt a strong hand on her shoulder and a vivid presence standing beside her—yet she was not afraid. The angelic being communicated to her that Heidi would know great pain and suffering but that she would be victorious. And then the lovely presence was gone. Heidi was fourteen years old at the time, and the mother pondered this message in her heart for about a year. But since everything seemed to be going well, it was soon forgotten.

Just before Heidi was to graduate from high school she came down with German measles, which turned into encephalitis (sleeping sickness.) This was followed by several long years of illness and much pain. Heidi's brain had swollen, and none of her glands functioned. She could only lie in bed day after day, year after year, in a dull, spiritless stupor. She gained weight until she weighed over 250 pounds, and it was nearly impossible for her mother to care for her.

After two years of saving every penny she could, Heidi's mother took her daughter to Mayo Clinic for ten days of intensive testing. When all the tests were completed the doctor told her firmly, but kindly, that she would have to put Heidi in an institution for the remainder of her life, as her brain and glands were destroyed.

But the mother could not do this. She took Heidi home and spent the long night praying and sobbing. The following evening she gathered her children around her and told them what the doctors had said. Remembering the message the angel had given her so many years earlier, she asked the children to join her in a prayer of relinquishment for Heidi. She knew she had done everything humanly possible for her daughter and the only thing left was to put her totally into the care of God who dearly loved her. She was certain God expected her to believe the message of the angel, so that night the mother and children prayed.

Ten days of internal bleeding followed this prayer, and then one day Heidi began to rally. Within six months she could walk, talk, and remember. Another few months passed and she could ride a bicycle and swim. Within the year she lost one hundred pounds and began to cook and laugh again. At the age of twenty-three she married a childhood sweetheart and they now have three beautiful children. Heidi began college after her children were in school and got her B.A. degree in nursing, making all A's in the process.

Heidi's family often speaks of the message of warning and hope brought to them by an angel so long ago and rejoices over the miracle of her recovery.

TWO-YEAR-OLD MARK was walking to the parking lot with his mother one Sunday after church and Sunday school when he tripped over a low cement wall and fell down. The fall wasn't serious but it scared him enough to cause him to cry. As his mother ran to pick him up, a man got there first and set Mark gently on his feet. He took a moment to wipe the tears from Mark's eyes and to talk to him. He was exceptionally tender with Mark and seemed full of compassion and love.

When Mark's mother turned to thank the man, no one was there. The thought flashed across her mind that the man must have been an angel—Mark's guardian angel. As she wondered why the Lord would send an angel for such a little fall, she remembered the verse, "Thy will be done on earth as it is in heaven," and thought to herself, "That's the way God's will is done, with love."

Mother and son went home from church that day with a feeling their lives had been brushed with a never-to-be-forgotten moment of glory.

At times God spoke to His servants in the Bible by sending an angel to them in a dream. The angel always conveyed a specific message from God, such as in the following story.

Pat IS A DEDICATED young minister with an abounding love for people and a zest for living. This joy is reflected in his relationship with his wife and baby son. Several years ago, before he was married, God taught Pat the important relationship between forgiveness and forgetting.

As a new Christian, the most difficult place for Pat to live out his new found faith in Jesus Christ was with his younger sister. She was just as new at being a Christian as he was, and they often used each other's faith as a reason to criticize the other's behavior. Pat was convinced his greatest calling in life was to be his sister's self-appointed judge, and he had become very proficient at that!

One night after an especially disagreeable confrontation with her, he had a dream that his sister had committed some shocking sin. He couldn't remember what it was but he remembers his feeling of extreme satisfaction because he had her cornered, and she was guilty. With genuine tears of repentance, his sister asked him to forgive her. Pat self-righteously said he would, but all the while he felt great pride because he definitely had the upper hand. At this point in his dream a magnificent angel with eyes like flaming stars appeared. The angel asked Pat if he would forgive his sister. Overwhelmed by this extraordinary, powerful presence, Pat answered meekly, "Yes." Then the angel asked him a question that has had a profound effect upon his life and ministry. "Will you forgive her *as if it never happened*?"

The words of the angel were indelibly impressed upon Pat's mind. And although he had that dream nine years ago, the intensity of the message is as clear as if it had happened last night. During these past years of ministry when he counsels someone, or when he himself has felt unjustly wronged, the angel's message has come back to him with clarity and force.

"Will you forgive as if it never happened?"

When the servant of the man of God got up and went out early the next morning, an army with horses and chariots had surrounded the city. "Oh, my lord, what shall we do?" the servant asked.

"Don't be afraid," the prophet answered. "Those who are with us are more than those who are with them."

And Elisha prayed, "O Lord, open his eyes so he may see." Then the Lord opened the servant's eyes, and he looked and saw the hills full of horses and chariots of fire all around Elisha.

2 Kings 6:15–17

LUIZ CAROLS GREW UP in the large city of São Paulo, Brazil. When he was in his early teens he committed his life to Jesus Christ. After many years of study he graduated from college and seminary. Luiz had a burden to reach the people in the interior of Brazil with the message of Jesus Christ, so he moved his family to one of the villages near the jungle.

Through the years many people in the village became Christians. This made the people in the neighboring village angry with the Christians, however, because they no longer traded with them in their idol-making. They vowed to come over the pass and kill them all.

The people in Luiz's village gathered together to pray about the situation. Days went by, then weeks—yet they never came. Several months later the chief of the warring village came over to talk to the mayor. The people gathered around him and asked why his village hadn't come and made war with them?

The chief said they had started across the pass but they were confronted by a large army with drawn swords on white horses blocking the way. Frightened, they had turned around and fled home.

IN SEPTEMBER OF 1971, Robbie, a serviceman
stationed at Clark Air Force base in Manila, Henry, a
missionary, and Tim, Henry's older son, had traveled from
Manila, Philippines, to the Naval Communications Station
in San Miguel. There they conducted a fellowship meeting
for the Christian servicemen on the base. It had rained hard
all that day and night and was still raining when they got
up the following morning to start back to Clark Air Force
Base.

The return trip over mountains and through flooded
valleys was tedious. The roads were gutted with deep
potholes filled with water, making driving extremely
dangerous. Soon they realized they could not go any farther
and stopped in a small, muddy village. Tim decided he had
to get back to the base so he waded out into the muddy
road, hoping to catch a bus. Robbie and Henry stayed with
the van. They were both soaking wet from the many times
along the way when they had to get out to push the car
through the mud. Everything inside the van was drenched
as well. They were totally miserable.

About nine o'clock that night they drove into an
all-night gas station, feeling it would be a fairly safe place,
and asked if they could park the van there until the next
morning. They were cold, hungry, and tired. Just as they
were ready to lie down on the wet seats and try to get some
sleep, they heard a knock. Robbie rolled down the window
and asked their visitor what he wanted. The man offered
them some girls. They told him they were Christians and
not interested in his offer. With this refusal, the man then
offered them some boys. When this was refused, too, the
man and his companion became very angry. They walked
around the van, kicking at it and shouting loudly that they
would be back. Robbie turned to Henry and said, "Brother,
I'm afraid. What should we do?"

"There isn't much we can do," Henry replied, trying
not to show his concern. "Let's just lock up the van tight

and try to get some sleep and trust God to take care of us."

After they had prayed together, Robbie stretched out on the back seat and Henry laid down on the front seat. Soon they were asleep.

The night passed and dawn came. The sun was shining and both of them were very hungry. Henry told Robbie he was going to find a place to eat and went to ask the station owner where they could buy some food.

She replied, "You can go around the corner and buy some baked goods at my father's bakery, but that isn't necessary because I've provided food here for you." She had food cooking on the burner, and a small table was set with six places.

"Go call your friends and you can all eat here," she said.

"Well, there are only two of us," Henry replied.

"But where are the others?" she asked. "There are supposed to be six of you."

Henry looked puzzled and said, "I don't know what you are talking about because there are only two of us. I'll go and call my friend."

The owner told him that the workers who kept the station open all night had seen four men with their arms folded, sitting up in the van all night long.

"They thought they were traveling companions of yours and your friend's," she explained. She called the night workers over and they assured her this was true.

Henry and Robbie were overwhelmed to think that angels had guarded their van while they slept.

JOHN IS AN AIRLINE PILOT today, but at one time he owned a gun shop. The store was in a small, isolated area of town. John was aware of the many problems that can arise from owning a gun shop, and one day he asked his pastor and one of the elders from church if they would come over and pray for the protection of the store. He asked them to pray that the people who came into his shop would not buy guns for the wrong purposes and that the store would be guarded from all evil.

One day a tough looking man came in to buy a gun. John noticed he was accompanied by several rough looking men riding their motorcycles around in front of his store. He felt the man had no good intentions in owning a gun and refused to sell him anything. The man was very angry when he left. The next day he returned with an equally tough looking friend, and they rode around the parking lot on their motorcycles most of the day, trying to intimidate John. John prayed and asked God to send His angels to protect him. After several hours of harassment, the men drove off and never returned.

Later that day a friend stopped by the shop to visit. He mentioned he had been by earlier but didn't come in. John asked him why he hadn't.

"Well, the inside of your shop was so full of customers I didn't want to bother you," he answered.

Yet no one had been in the store all that day!

Today as John pilots his big 727 across the starry heavens, he is conscious of a higher glory that surrounds him. He is reminded of the great privilege God's children have in asking for protection in times of danger.

Paul was a successful lawyer in Southern India. One day a client shared with him the story of God's love and the message of salvation. Paul bowed his head in his office and committed his life to Jesus Christ. A few years later he felt God wanted him to become a full-time missionary. He moved with his family to the northern part of India. He spent his first few months in his new surroundings getting to know the people and longing for the day when he could set up a tent and hold daily Bible studies.

At last that time came. The tent was put up with much joy. Not very many came at first; but as time went on, it became the gathering place for everyone in the village. Many committed their lives to Jesus Christ and began to live for Him. But others were opposed to what Paul was doing and decided he should leave.

One night as Paul was walking home after the meeting, the opposition group was waiting for him and began to beat him up, driving their punches home with brutal force. Paul's nose was broken as he was knocked to the ground. But suddenly a small band of people surrounded him, and those who were trying to beat him could not get through the circle. To Paul's utter amazement his tormentors ran off. When he turned to thank the people who had protected him, no one was there.

Paul was never troubled again and God greatly blessed his ministry in the years ahead. He is convinced the small group of people that protected him that night was a band of heavenly angels sent by God.

BORN IN RUSSIA many years ago, Al felt secure and loved in the small village where he grew up with his family and most of his relatives. He had a happy childhood until one day he noticed his parents seemed sorrowful and frightened. He had been aware of an oppressive atmosphere in his home and throughout the village; but when he saw his mother put a few belongings into a large cloth and tie up the four corners, and when he heard the words "flee" and "escape," he sensed something ominous was about to happen. His father sat down with him one evening and explained it was imperative for their family, along with about one hundred others, to leave Russia. Al was too young to understand why.

Early the following morning, long before the sun was up, they left their home and the little village with its many happy memories. A few days later the Russian Army found out about their escape and, with trained dogs, rode off in search of the small band of people. When Al's father saw the soldiers approaching in the distance, he ordered the entire group to lie down, single file, in a deep crevice along the side of the road. To the complete amazement of the frightened group, they heard the army and the howling dogs ride right past them. Al's parents and several others looked up and discovered why. A band of angels stood between them and the soldiers. Every person in that little fleeing group escaped to safety.

Today Al is head of a mission that has an important ministry with people behind the iron curtain. He faces many dangers in his work, but he has a courageous faith that comes from the certain knowledge that God's angels protect His children many times during life.

After the Sabbath, at dawn on the first day of the week, Mary Magdalene and the other Mary went to look at the tomb.

There was a violent earthquake, for an angel of the Lord came down from heaven and, going to the tomb, rolled back the stone and sat on it. His appearance was like lightning, and his clothes were white as snow. The guards were so afraid of him that they shook and became like dead men.

The angel said to the women, "Do not be afraid, for I know that you are looking for Jesus, who was crucified. He is not here; he has risen, just as he said. Come and see the place where he lay.

Matt. 28:1–6

Many people shared stories about the appearance of an angel at the time of death. Through reading these experiences, we are reminded again of the truth that Christians do not walk across the valley of the shadow of death alone. God sends His angels to escort us into His presence.

BILL'S FATHER WAS DYING. Although he was in his late 80's, Bill knew he would be left with a feeling of deep loss when his father was gone. Late one night Bill was called to the small community hospital to spend the last moments of his father's life at his bedside. Tears rolled unashamedly down his cheeks as he looked at the gentle, lined face of his father. He remembered the days when his dad had been a vibrant, energetic doctor who had a kind word for everyone. Suddenly his father opened his eyes and said in his firm, clear voice of years ago, "Bill, I hear the most beautiful choir of angels singing. Oh! Do you hear it too?" And then Bill saw an angel, outlined in silver, standing by the bed between him and his father. This amazingly beautiful being filled the room with an intense feeling of love and peace such as he had never experienced. Bill looked at his father's face and saw that it was every bit as radiant and glowing as the angel who stood by his bed. A few moments later his father went to be with the Lord.

Bill sat for a long time in the quietness of the room. The peace and love that had accompanied the angel lingered with him for as long as he remained in the room. And although it has dimmed with the passing of years, Bill knows that time can never fully erase that golden glimpse he had into eternity.

JIM GREEN WAS A young boy attending a Catholic grade school. As he walked to school each day, he always paused a moment in front of the old graystone church to look at his favorite pictures, a series of pastel paintings of angels, full of radiant splendor and glory, blowing their trumpets. A quick shudder of wonder always passed through his body as he tried to imagine what it would be like to hear the sound of the angels' trumpets. Would they roar like the north wind, filling the entire earth with a triumphant blast of victory? Or would they be soft and melodious like the sound of a golden harp?

One day after helping to serve an early Mass, Jim went to talk to his old priest. He asked whether or not angels were real.

As Jim sat down with Father Joseph Reddin, the priest put his hand on Jim's head and said, "Young man, I am going to tell you a story about a dear friend of mine. She was a godly woman and I went to her home every day to see her because she was in failing health. On one particular day my visit was not routine because I was told she was failing quickly and might be going to be with the Lord right away. As I went to her home and walked into her bedroom, I saw her lying there with a bright shining face. I sat down next to her and held her hand and asked her what this incredible sense of new strength was that she had. In a weakened voice she said, 'Father, the angels have been hovering around this morning and have been taking care of all my uncertainties. My new strength is the hope that comes from God that the angels have brought to me.'"

Father Reddin told Jim that in many instances when he performed last rites, the dying people have shared this same sense of certainty, that they were being ministered to by angels sent from God. Father Reddin described the peace that filled their hearts as every need was met and all their earthly concerns vanished.

Today Jim, in his mid-forties, serves the Lord in

Monterey, California. But he has never forgotten the story the old priest took time to tell him as a young, inquiring boy. Nor has he forgotten the tinge of excitement that filled his heart from that day forward each time he stopped to look at the pastel paintings on the front of the old church building of the angels blowing their trumpets.

MARTHA'S MOTHER LAY DYING after several months of prolonged suffering. As Martha sat by her bed one day, they spent a lovely time sharing quietly together many happy events from their lives. Suddenly her mother sat straight up in bed and, with a voice full of joy, said, "I see my mother and father!" She paused for a moment and then, with a smile of incomparable beauty, added, "And I see Jesus! He's motioning for me to come toward them— and oh, Martha, I see the most beautiful angels!"

With a look of radiance Martha had never seen, her mother lay back on the pillow and died.

The room became quiet and bathed in peace. A warm ray of comfort, like a touch of golden sunshine, filled Martha's heart that day and has remained with her ever since.

As A NURSE, Joy had seen many patients die. It was always difficult for her, but she knew one case she was working on would be especially painful. Her patient was a thirty-five-year-old mother. Joy was in the room with her during her dying moments. Her two little children, ages six and nine, were standing at her bedside with wide, fearful eyes. This lovely Christian mother left her children a legacy of hope and joy that will remain with them forever.

Moments before she died, she described to her children the angels who had come to escort her into the presence of the King. It was the most positive approach to help children cope with death Joy had ever witnessed. The mother described the cheerful, healthy looking young angels who were holding her hands and telling her how excited God was to have her come home.

"The angels tell me there is a special house there just for me. The floors never need waxing; so when you come to join me, I won't complain if you spill your Kool-Aid. And there's a choir for me to sing in—and my seat is in the front row! And oh, the angels tell me Jesus is waiting at the front door—for me! I've made my angels promise to watch over you both and bring you to Jesus, too. These angels are so nice and *happy*!" she told them.

And with that, she went Home to be with the Lord.

The following two stories are almost identical. Yet I have heard reports exactly like them from people all over the world. One was recently announced over CBS Evening News in Chicago. Most were told to me by those I know and greatly respect.

I believe there are times in history when God sends messengers to announce the approaching of a new era or historical event. This happened when the angels announced the birth of Jesus, His resurrection, and His ascension. It could be that we are about to enter the period of history when the Lord Jesus Christ will return. It is possible He is sending His messengers to various people throughout the world to alert us.

The first time I heard this story was fourteen years ago, when my husband and I were missionaries in Brazil. It was told to us by one of the most respected Brazilian ministers we had the privilege of knowing.

Rev. RICADO WAS DRIVING his car down a red dusty road in Brazil on his way to call on a sick member of his church. It was a fifteen-mile trip through the mato, a rather desolate stretch of barren land. He saw a young hitchhiker beside the road and stopped to pick him up. As they drove along, Rev. Ricado began to share with the young man about the love of Jesus.

"I believe the Lord's return is getting close," Rev. Ricado said during the conversation.

"Well, that may be sooner than you think," the young man answered softly, much to Rev. Ricado's surprise.

When Rev. Ricado turned to look at him, the young man was gone. He stopped the car, looked up and down the lonely road, but could see no one in any direction.

A SEMINARY PROFESSOR and his wife were touring the beautiful northwest last summer with another couple. They saw a woman standing by the side of the road who looked like she might need help, so they stopped to pick her up. She seemed to be exceptionally intelligent and had an unusual air of peace and authority about her. They all began to talk about Mt. St. Helens and the many other phenomena of nature that seemed to be occurring around the world.

"It seems like things are heading up for the return of the Lord," the professor said.

"That may be sooner than you think," the woman responded. And then she was gone. The four friends were so shocked they could hardly believe what had happened. They stopped the car and looked up and down the road, but there was no sign of her.

When they arrived at the next town, they stopped at the police station to report the incident. The rugged looking sergeant was sitting behind the desk, working on some papers, when the professor walked up to him.

"I have something strange to tell you," he said. "I'm sure you won't believe me, but we were driving along and stopped to pick up a woman who looked like she needed help." He continued to tell the officer all that had happened. When he finished his story, the officer looked up at him.

"Well, I have something just as strange to tell you," he said. "You're the seventh person driving through town to turn in a report like this in the last twenty-four hours."

I was surprised at the number of stories I received from people who had seen and heard a choir of angels. I was reminded of the passage in Luke 2 in which the angels appeared to the shepherds. "Suddenly an angel appeared among them, and the landscape shone bright with the glory of the Lord. They were badly frightened, but the angel reassured them. 'Don't be afraid!' he said. 'I bring you the most joyful news ever announced, and it is for everyone! The Savior . . . has been born tonight in Bethlehem! . . .' Suddenly, the angel was joined by a vast host of others—the armies of heaven—praising God: 'Glory to God in the highest heaven,' they sang, 'and peace on earth for all those pleasing him'" (Luke 2:9–14 LB).

My last story tells of the angels' song.

DAVID WAS THE PASTOR of a fairly new church in Hawaii. One day while preparing his sermon for the following Sunday, he felt constrained to call the other two pastors who served with him to go into the church and pray together. He was deeply concerned that the church was not growing the way he knew it should. There were so many people in the area who desperately needed the Savior's touch on their lives.

The three pastors knelt down in front of the church and began to pray for the people on that beautiful paradise island. God had given them a message of love and forgiveness and hope, yet something was missing. Their hearts cried out for help. As they passed into the second hour of prayer together, suddenly the church was filled with beautiful music that sounded like waves breaking gently along the shore. He turned around to look, and to his utter astonishment he saw the church filled with a gloriously shining choir of angels. He thought he must be seeing things and stopped the prayer. He asked the other two pastors if they heard any music. When they turned around, they too saw the shining beauty of the angelic choir. The three ministers fell on their faces as the music grew louder and louder. At last it became a triumphant song of joy and praise, pealing through the church and singing its way into their very hearts and souls. As the angels sang praises to the King, the pastors had an unbearable longing to join them. Then the music died away, leaving behind only the heavenly echoes of memory.

As they continued to kneel in trembling awe, they were filled with an overwhelming sense of glory and worship. In the intensity of the moment, David realized that he had been omitting the supernatural element of God from his preaching.

A quietness filled the pastors' hearts and a feeling of deep peace and wonder swept over them like waves from some faraway ocean shore. They left the church with a revitalized message of the power and glory of God.

Jesus did many other miraculous signs in the presence of his disciples, which are not recorded in this book. But these are written that you may believe that Jesus is the Christ, the Son of God, and that by believing you may have life in his name.

John 20:30–31

Part 3

GOD'S CALL– OUR RESPONSE

God's Call—
Our Response

GOD'S CALL

God calls us to be His messengers. We are angels "with skin on," as the little boy said in the story. He sends us out each day to be physical "angels of mercy" to those around us who are in need. This is illustrated in the following story.

Katharina was dying of cancer. She was bedridden in her home. I watched as a small band of human "angels" went every day to minister to her. They bathed her, dressed her open wound, fed her, read to her, prayed with her and for her, and sat quietly beside her. They cleaned her house, prepared her food, and washed the clothes. They brought comfort, peace, and joy to her and to her husband, Paul. They continued this ministry of love, day after day, for over nine months. I wasn't a bit surprised when I heard that just before Katharina died she saw a band of heavenly angels standing by, ready to escort her into the presence of her

Lord and Savior. For nine months she had been surrounded by some of God's faithful, human "angels," and the transition between the two realms is really very small.

God is calling each one of us to be His messengers of love to a lost, suffering world. He is calling us to bring hope to the hopeless and to bind up the brokenhearted. This starts where we live, with those nearest us: husband, wife, children, parents, roommate. God calls us to go out into the world and demonstrate His love to everyone with whom we come in contact. How are we responding to His call today?

When I think of a human "angel," I am often reminded of my friend Frieda Bowker. There is a joyful beauty about her that touches every area of her life. She is from Switzerland, and although she lives in Seattle, she has transported the Swiss love of flowers into her own home. The moment you drive into her driveway, you feel you have entered an enchanted garden. The scent of flowers fills the air with sweet perfume. There are drifts of marigolds, daffodils, and forget-me-nots. And roses stand in majestic splendor, alive with the colors of the rainbow. The beauty of Frieda's garden is carried over into her floral paintings. They bring a touch of sunshine to every home in which they are displayed. They, too, are a reflection of God's love in Frieda's heart. She has found many creative ways to demonstrate this love. For example, each week when she calls on the sick she picks a small bouquet of her flowers and ties them up with a pretty bow of lace. When she walks into the hospital room in her quiet, reticent manner, her face breaks into a radiant smile as she hands the flowers to the patient. She doesn't stay long, just long enough to bring the gift of love. There are times when Frieda is sad, hurt, and disappointed with life. But like all of us, she is simply an earthen vessel who holds within her the matchless gift of God's love. Still, she has found ways to respond to the call of God and to become His messenger in a destitute world.

OUR RESPONSE

We must always bear in mind that there is an immense difference between God's heavenly angels and ourselves. God never created us to be angels. He created us to have a relationship with Him—a relationship so close and personal that we can become His beloved children. "Yet to all who received him, to those who believed in his name, he gave the right to become children of God—" (John 1:12). Not only are we God's children, but we are permitted to call this great, omnipotent, God-Creator-Redeemer our Father! When Jesus taught the disciples to pray, He taught them to say, "Our Father in Heaven." When we add to that prodigious truth the astonishing fact that we are called heirs of God and joint heirs with Christ, we begin to catch an infinitesimal glimpse of the holy position into which God has placed us.

> The Spirit himself testifies with our spirit that we are God's children. Now if we are children, then we are heirs—heirs of God and co-heirs with Christ, if indeed we share in his sufferings in order that we may also share in his glory (Rom. 8:16, 17).

No, we are not God's heavenly angels, rather we are God's children and heirs. We come to Him as a child, and say with a full heart, "Father, my Father." "You have been adopted into the very family circle of God whereby you cry with a full heart, "Abba, Father" (Rom. 8:16 PHILLIPS).

When my husband and I visited Israel a few years ago, we became good friends with our tour guide, Baruch. He and Harry spent many hours together. They learned to regard one another with deep respect. One afternoon Baruch invited us to his home for tea. It was an honor for us to be in an Israeli home. His lovely wife had prepared many delicious baked goods for us, and we had a delightful time together. Suddenly, his little eight-year-old daughter came bursting into the room. She had not been with her father for several days and was overjoyed to see him again. She ran straight across the room into his waiting arms crying, "Abba! Abba! Abba!" Harry and I smiled as we watched this happy reunion. But something else happened, too. Our hearts skipped a beat in electric excitement because we had never heard anyone call their father "Abba" before. We only knew that name from the Bible. Later Harry asked Baruch what "Abba" actually meant.

"Abba is the most endearing term a child can call his/her father. It is perhaps similar to your word for daddy, or papa," Baruch told us.

That verse we had memorized so long ago took on new meaning for us that day. To think we had the right, as God's children, to call Him "Papa," or "Daddy." There will never be a more beautiful truth than that. "How great is the love the Father has lavished on us, that we should be called children of God! And that is what we are!" (1 John 3:1).

No, we are not angels. We may carry out some of the work the angels do as God's messengers; but we will never be angels because we are called to be God's beloved children.

In the Hebrew language, there is no word for "thank you." When someone does something nice for another, gratitude is expressed by a word which means "I will honor your name. I will make your name known." This is the way we should thank God for all He has done for us. "Lord, because of your great love for me, I accept your Son, Jesus Christ, as my Savior, and will honor your name through my life—the way I live each day in my home, at work, at school, in the hospital, in prison, at play, or wherever I might be."

This is our response in answer to God's call for us to become His children. And the angels in Heaven can never fully understand this because they can never know the joy that our salvation brings in Christ Jesus our Lord.

There is rejoicing in the presence of the angels of God over one sinner who repents.

Luke 15:10

Biblical Angel References*

Angel

Genesis
16:7-11
21:17
22:11
22:15
24:7
24:40
31:11
48:16

Exodus
3:2
14:19
23:20
23:23
32:34
33:2

Numbers
20:16
22:22
22:23-35

Judges
2:1

2:4
5:23
6:11
6:12
6:20
6:21
6:22
13:3
13:6
13:16
15:17
13:18-21

1 Samuel
29:9

2 Samuel
14:17
14:20
19:27
24:16
24:17

1 Kings
13:18
19:5
19:7

2 Kings
1:3
1:15
19:35

1 Chronicles
21:12
21:15
21:16
21:18
21:20
21:27
21:30

2 Chronicles
32:21

Psalms
34:7
35:5
35:6

Ecclesiastes
5:6

Isaiah
37:36
63:9

*These references were taken from James Strong, *Strong's Exhaustive Concordance of the Bible,* rev. ed. Nashville: Abingdon, 1980.

Daniel
3:28
6:22

Hosea
12:4

Zechariah
1:9
1:11
1:12
1:13
1:14
1:19
2:3
3:1
3:3
3:5
3:6
4:1
4:4
4:5
5:5
5:10
6:4
4:5
14:8

Matthew
1:20
1:24
2:13
2:19
28:2
28:5

Luke
1:11
1:13
1:18
1:19
1:26
1:28
1:30
1:35
1:38
2:9

2:10
2:13
2:21
22:43

John
5:4
12:29

Acts
5:19
6:15
7:30
7:35
7:38
8:26
10:3
10:7
10:22
11:13
12:7
12:8
12:9
12:10
12:11
12:15
12:23
23:8
23:9
27:23

1 Corinthians
11:14

Galatians
1:8
4:14

Revelation
1:1
2:1
2:8
2:12
2:18
3:1
3:7
3:14

5:2
7:2
8:3
8:5
8:7
8:8
8:10
8:12
8:13
9:1
9:11
9:13
9:14
10:1
10:5
10:7
10:8
10:9
11:1
11:15
14:6
14:8
14:9
14:15, 17
14:18
14:19
16:3
16:4
16:5
16:8
16:10
16:12
16:17
17:7
18:1
18:2
19:17
20:1
21:17
22:6
22:8
22:16

Angel's
Revelation
8:4
10:10

124

Notes

[1]Billy Graham, *Angels, God's Secret Agents,* (New York: Doubleday, 1975), p. 8.

[2]Peter Lamborn Wilson, *Angels,* (New York: Pantheon, 1980), p. 34.

[3]Fred C. Dickason, *Angels, Elect and Evil,* (Chicago: Moody, 1975), p. 13.

[4]Johnson Oatman, Jr., and J.R. Sweney, *"Holy Holy Is What the Angels Sing."*

Bibliography

Dickason, C. Fred. *Angels Elect and Evil*. Chicago: Moody, 1975.
Graham, Billy. *Angels, God's Secret Agents*. New York: Doubleday, 1975.
International Standard Bible Encyclopedia. Grand Rapids: Eerdmans, 1939.
Interpreter's Dictionary of the Bible. New York: Abingdon, 1962.
Leavell, Landrum P. *Angels, Angels, Angels*. Nashville: Broadman, 1973.
Lewis, C.S. *The Problem of Pain*. New York: Macmillan, 1962.
Miller, Leslie C. *All About Angels*. New York: Pyramid Publications, Pyramid Books, 1973.
Smith, Hannah Whitall. *The God of All Comfort*. Chicago: Moody, 1956.
Strong, James, S.T.D., Lld. Nashville: Abingdon-Cokesbury Press, 1890.
Swinhart, Stephen D. *Angels in Heaven and Earth*. Plainfield: Logos International, 1979.
Wilson, Peter Lamborn. *Angels*. New York: Pantheon, 1980.
Yancey, Philip. *Where is God When It Hurts?* Grand Rapids, Zondervan, 1977.
Zondervan Pictorial Encyclopedia of the Bible. Grand Rapids: Zondervan, 1975.